# Changing the Picture

## How to Stay Motivated Series
## Book 3

# Zig Ziglar

Made for Success
PUBLISHING

Made for Success Publishing
P.O. Box 1775 Issaquah, WA 98027
www.MadeForSuccessPublishing.com

Distributed by Made for Success Publishing

**Library of Congress Cataloging-in-Publication data**
Ziglar, Zig
Changing the Picture: How to Stay Motivated Book 3

p. cm.

LCCN: 2020940767
ISBN: 978-1-61339-746-6  (Paperback)
ISBN: 978-1-64146-542-7  (Audiobook)
ISBN: 978-1-64146-541-0  (eBook)

Printed in the United States of America

For further information contact Made for Success Publishing
+14255266480 or email service@madeforsuccess.net

# TABLE OF CONTENTS

# 1

# WINNERS RESPOND—
# NOT REACT

Throughout this book, I will talk a great deal about the importance of what I like to call "changing your picture." Positive thinking won't work unless you have a good, solid picture of yourself. Therefore, you need to begin to build a healthy self-image to make a difference in your life. In this first chapter, you're going to learn how to get along with yourself, which is key to getting along with others. We will look at the causes of poor self-image, the manifestations of that poor self-image, and, most importantly, what you can do about it.

Us fellas, we frequently kid the ladies about gossiping. As I walked into the office building this morning, however, I saw a couple of *guys* talking. I heard one of them say, "I can't tell you any more. I've already told you more than I heard!"

This gossip-like conversation seems to be a trend, unfortunately.

As I continued into work, a couple of ladies were talking. As I walked past, one of them exclaimed, "There's Zig!"

The other one said, "Yeah! You know, I'd rather hear that guy talk than eat."

The other one replied, "Me too. I've heard him eat!"

## The Initial Question

The question I want to start with is this: Do you respond to life, or do you react to life?

Doctors say that to *respond* is positive, while to *react* is negative. For example, when you get sick, you go to the doctor. She gives you a prescription and says, "See me tomorrow." When you walk in the next day, she will do one of two things. She might shake her head and say, "Uh-oh. Your body is *reacting* to the medicine; we have to change the prescription." Alternately, if she smiles and says, "Hey! It's working! Your body is *responding* to the treatment!" You know that everything's gonna be okay. The difference between responding and reacting is enormously important.

> **The choice to have a great attitude is something nobody or no circumstance can take from you.**

The choice to have a great attitude is something nobody or no circumstance can take from you.

Now, I'll give you an example of when I responded rather than reacted. On January 23rd,

1981, I was in Kansas City, Missouri. It was my final stop after a long week. Throughout the week, I had been doing four-hour seminars in the North, South, East, West, from border to border, and from coast to coast. When I do four-hour seminars, I expend an incredible amount of energy. On this particular day, we were recording. When you record, you turn it up a notch because you don't have your body to communicate with—it's got to be all voice and inflection and excitement—so I did just that.

Our recording gear back in 1981 was bulky. One of our recording boxes weighed over a hundred and forty pounds. My son-in-law, Chad Witmeyer, was helping me record. We had a three o'clock flight back to Dallas. The airline had said, "Hey, you gotta be here at least an hour early so we can stow the gear." So, the minute I finished, we started assembling, packing up as quickly as was humanly possible. We made the mad dash to the airport, and we got there at two o'clock.

When I walked into the airport, there were two long lines of people. We chose what I thought was the shortest line and prepared to wait. Almost immediately, I noticed a vacant spot down at the counter with a sign that said: "Position Closed." I also noticed a lady walking around behind the counter. I knew in my mind that in a matter of minutes, "Position Closed" would be turned over to "Position Open." I got ready. Sure enough, the lady walked down, flipped the sign over, looked at the two long lines of people and announced, "Those of you who have a seat on the three o'clock flight to Dallas, come over here."

Quick as a flash, I was over there. I mean, I got to the new line before anybody else had even left the old line. The lady smiled at me ever-so-pleasantly and said, "The three o'clock flight to Dallas has been canceled."

I said, "Faaaan-tastic!"

She looked at me strangely and said, "Whaddya mean, fantastic? I just told you your flight has been canceled."

I answered, "Ma'am, it's very simple. There are only three reasons on earth why anybody would ever cancel a flight to Dallas, Texas. Number one: something is wrong with that airplane. Number two: something is wrong with the person who's going to fly that airplane. Number three: something is wrong way up there! Now, ma'am, if any one of those three situations exists, I don't want to be up there. I want to be right down here! Fantastic."

Now, have you ever noticed that some people can't wait to give you bad news? "Aw, Sally, I hate to tell you this. It just kills me to tell you this!" They can't wait to get the bad news out. The woman at the airline counter put her hands on her hips and retorted, "Yeah. But the next flight doesn't leave until six!"

I said, "Fannnn-tastic!"

By now, the other long lines of people were looking over at me as if to say, "Who is that nut that says everything is fantastic?"

It brought the gate agent to a dead stop. She looked at me and she said, "Now, look. I just told you that you've got a four-hour wait here in the Kansas City airport. You said 'fantastic!' Now, why on earth would you say a thing like that?"

"Ma'am, it's very simple. I'm fifty-four years old, and in my lifetime, I have never before had an opportunity to spend four hours in the airport in Kansas City, Missouri. Do you realize at this precise moment, there are literally tens of millions of people on the face of this earth who are not only cold but also hungry? Although it is awfully cold on the outside, here I am in a marvelously warm building. There's a nice little coffee shop down the way. I'm going to go down there, get myself a cup of coffee, and relax for a minute. Then, I've got some extremely important work I've got to do. Here I am in one of the most beautiful buildings in the Kansas City area, with four hours of rent-free space, and I am really excited about it!"

Now, you might be thinking to yourself, "Ziglar, I've heard about these positive thinkers, but man, that's kind of way out! Are you telling me the truth? Are you absolutely sure that's exactly what you said—Scout's honor?"

That is exactly what I said, and my son-in-law will validate that statement.

"Okay, okay! You said it! But now, tell me the truth, Ziglar. Is that the way you really *felt*?"

Why, of course not! I'd been gone all week. I was tired. I wanted to be headed home. But you see, there are some things we absolutely are *not* going to change in our lives. Here, I had a choice. I didn't know that lady. I did, however, know that she could cancel my flight—but she couldn't cancel my day.

Did I want to respond, or did I want to react?

I could have reacted sarcastically. I could have thrown a temper-tantrum. "That's great! That's just great. I've had my seat reserved for over a month now. I've had my ticket for nearly a month! As I drove up here, I couldn't help but notice a whole bunch of your airplanes sitting out there on the runway, not doing a cotton-pickin' thing. Now, how come you can't crank up one of those airplanes and take me on down to Dallas?"

I could have said all that. You know what? The next flight would have still left at six.

I could have jumped up and down, ranted and raved, screamed and stomped my feet, made an absolute idiot out of myself, and demanded my rights. "I'll sue you, that's what I'll do! Do you hear me? I will sue you for such a dastardly deed you're pulling here!"

And the next flight would have still left at six.

There are some things you aren't going to change. If you were born white, you're going to stay white. If you were born black, you're going to stay black. You're not going to change one whisper about yesterday. But tomorrow is an entirely different story! Whether you respond or react to life determines exactly what is going to happen in the rest of your life.

> **You're not going to change one whisper about yesterday. But tomorrow is an entirely different story!**

As I said, that lady could cancel my flight; however, she could not cancel my day. You know how folks are. You allow them to cancel one day, and the next thing you know, they'll want to cancel two days, three days, and then four days. Some people, ladies and gentlemen, permit others to cancel their lifetime. I've seen it happen. Do you respond to life? Or do you react to life? These are enormously important questions we need to answer.

Have you ever been driving down the freeway, minding your own business, when all of a sudden, some idiot pulls in front of you? You slam on your brakes, you hit your horn, and you give him a piece of your mind. "Why don't you watch where you're goin', ya' dummy! I could'a hit you, and I could'a been killed. You could'a been killed, too! I'm telling you. Your life is not safe anymore!" I mean, you really read him the riot act. You get down to the office, and you tell the first person you meet about "these crazy people on the freeway." You tell everyone. "Musta' been drunk or on drugs or something! Life is not safe anymore!"

In the meantime, the man who did the dastardly deed rides merrily along, unaware of your existence. Yet, he's in control of your thinking. This means he's also in control of your actions. He is affecting your relationship with those below you, above you, and around you, which means he is ultimately in control of your career. You don't even know who he is! This is the ultimate put-down. Here, do you respond? Or do you react to life? Your self-image is the key to which one you do. Does every little thing that comes along threaten you? Or do you respond to these situations?

Several years ago, I went to the North Dallas bank. As I was pulling out into the flow of traffic, I only did it half-right, turning my head only to the right. All of a sudden, I heard the screeching of brakes and the shriek of an extraordinarily large horn. I hit my brakes as quickly as I could. I looked up just in time to see this dude come steaming by in a big Mercedes. If the look he gave me could have killed, there would've been a funeral in Dallas a couple of days later. If his look could have melted steel, I would have needed a new automobile. I have never seen such a high concentration of ugly in one spot in my life. That dude was upset.

Now, you see, I had a choice. I could have looked at him and screamed, "Why don't you watch where *you're* goin', ya' dummy? I could've been killed, too. Come on back here, and we'll talk about this thing!"

Suppose he had? Suppose he'd come back, gotten out, and beaten me up? Folks, this is both kind of funny and tragically serious. Every day of our lives in America, people are killed for lesser reasons than that. People react; they don't respond.

I had a choice: do I respond to what just happened, or do I react? As he rode past, I looked up at him and said, "Hi!" I did a double-take, and he smiled big. He waved his hand back at me, probably thinking, "Boy, I almost blew it! That must be a friend of mine!"

I believe it is infinitely more important to respond than to react. This response is going to play a major role in how you get along with your mate, your children, your boss, your employees, your next-door-neighbor, and everybody else. The key to responding correctly lies in your self-image.

The major point I want to make is this: you cannot tailor-make the situations in your life, but you can tailor-make your attitude to fit all situations in life. This attitude rests purely on the image you have of yourself.

What does this story have to do with your self-image? It has everything to do with it. Reaction breeds anger. It breeds depression. It breeds negativity and bitterness. Responding breeds hope and creativity. It breeds action.

## The Responder Versus the Reactor

I'd like to give you two classic examples of what I'm talking about. One is of a person who responded; the other offers a person who reacted.

A number of years ago, a lady who had built the sales management team within a particular company had a little problem with management. For whatever reason, management suddenly decided they needed to serve drinks—cocktails, beer, wine, and so forth—at their meetings, and particularly often at their regional and national conventions. She protested very strongly because she knew the destructiveness of alcohol. Her belief system simply said, "This is not a good idea." As a matter of fact, management was so unhappy with her resistance that, one morning, she awakened to find her desk on her front porch. After a number of years, she had been summarily fired.

This is a pretty drastic action. Now, this woman had a choice. Should she respond to this situation, or should she react to the situation? She very quickly analyzed the situation, realized she had already built the million-dollar organization, and decided she could do exactly the same thing for herself. So, she started a similar company. At the time, this was very difficult because bankers did not believe in loaning money to women—especially women who didn't believe in drinking. Beyond her thoughts of drinking, she had some weird ideas. For example, she thought you ought to pay your bills on time. She thought the customer should get a good deal, the salespeople should get a good deal, and the company still ought to be able to make a profit. She had a lot of strange ideas. She had a tough time, but she hung in there because she knew she was born to win.

The lady I'm talking about is Mary Crowley. The company I'm talking about is Home Interiors and Gifts. At the time of this writing, Mary's company did over 600 million dollars' worth of business. Mary responded to the situation; she did not react to the situation. Responding is incredibly important. It's a direct reflection of the picture you have of yourself.

A few months ago, I was in a meeting with a very strong, very successful businessman. This man started talking about his childhood, about how he was raised during World War II. His dad had gone off to war. While he was gone, his mother and aunt had made a "sissy" of their little boy. This, at least, was the word used by his father after he arrived home. What his father did as a result was very simple. He got a traveling job. Every Friday evening, he would come in and demand a list of all of the sins and crimes this little guy had committed in the weeks' absence. One by one, he would go down the list, forcing the youngster to fear every week when his dad returned home. On one memorable occasion during the first grade, a bully jumped the boy on the way to school and beat him up. The boy came home crying. His daddy pointed his finger and said to him, "If you gonna act like a girl, I'm gonna dress you like a girl." He actually put a dress on his son and sent him back out to fight the bully.

As I sat there listening and watching him, the tears were just streaming down his face. As he spoke, he said, "You know, I believe—I don't believe, I know—that that's one of the reasons I became an alcoholic." Then he summed it up with these words: "Long ago, I dealt with these issues. You see, I know my daddy did not treat me that way because he hated me. My daddy treated me that way because he loved me. That's exactly the way he had been raised. That was the only thing he knew. I've been able to deal with it and put it behind me."

Allow me to inject something important here. Most people don't do what they do because they want to hurt people. They do it because that's the best information they have to make their decisions. We need to understand that. We need to know this in order to make forgiveness easier. I'll get into this in greater detail later on. While Mary Crowley *responded,* this other gentleman initially *reacted,* which led to disastrous results.

## Understanding Your Self-Image

One of the most beautiful letters I've ever received is from a psychologist named Dr. Jocelyn Fuller. She'd recently attended a sales seminar, and she wrote, "You know, I never realized that salespeople are such good psychologists. I learned some things at a sales seminar that I never dreamed of knowing. I learned to appreciate my own profession more. Since then, I no longer have to parade my credentials. I no longer have to tell people all about my academic background. I still have 'em up on the wall, but I value myself for who I am and not because of some piece of paper or degree." I found this information enormously exciting!

One of the psychologists I work with is a man named Dr. John Leddo. Dr. Leddo says that if we treated every person like they were our best friend, we would be able to get along with far more people, be accepted by a whole lot more people, and substantially improve our own self-image as a result.

I know it's awfully tough to respond well when your mate of seventeen years walks out and leaves you with four children. You can't solve this in twenty minutes. I know it's tough to respond when a trusted friend and partner embezzles funds from the company, forces you into bankruptcy, and makes you lose your home. I know it's tough to respond when you're unjustly fired, when you were abused as a child, or when your child was killed by a drunk driver who then walked away, scot-free. It's an awfully tough thing to do. But the question is, how, exactly, do you respond? What are the steps you take?

First of all, you must acknowledge where you are. That's one of the things we often don't do because we don't want to think about it. Where are you when something bad like that happens? I'm here to tell you: we grow in adversity. Mary Crowley grew in adversity at her workplace. You can grow in adversity.

In the March 28th, 1993 issue of *Parade* magazine, there was an article on a young Fort Worth man named Randy Souder. At one time, he was seventeen years old, an athlete; he was a very healthy, outgoing young man. Unfortunately, he injured himself in a diving accident and became a paraplegic. He was in the hospital for five months. He was, of course, very upset about what had happened. One day, he was active and enthusiastic, doing everything a healthy seventeen-year-old athlete would do. The next moment, he realized he was going to be in a wheelchair for the rest of his life.

Naturally, Souder had a pity party for about five months there. But in the past, however, he had demonstrated some artistic skills. One of the therapists at the hospital forced a brush into his hand, and he started doing some artwork. After this, his objective was to get into creative advertising at an ad agency. When he began work, a gentleman at the ad agency saw one of his paintings and said, "Hey, do you have another picture like that? Do you have any that are for sale?"

Six years later, Souder had developed a talent that brought his paintings to over 1,500 galleries around the country. "Had this not happened to me, I doubt I would be where I am today," he said. He took the proverbial lemon; he made the proverbial lemonade. He took what happened to him, and he decided, "I got to get on with life."

People asked him, "Do you think about that wheelchair all the time?"

He responded, "The last thing I ever think about when I get up in the morning is my wheelchair. I'm excited about what I'm doin'."

When we get excited about life, we can respond to it instead of reacting *from* it.

But you must understand where you are. Take a little inventory. If you're feeling down, if you're really not happy with things, it's okay to get down.

In the February 3rd, 1987 issue of *The New York Times,* for example, they printed a very significant article. It pointed out that a lot of people have every reason to be negative and pessimistic. Their lives have indicated to them that, yes, that's where they ought to be. What we need to ask ourselves is, "In what state would I be had I faced some of those situations?"

But, the article also went on to say that once you have identified where you are in your life, you shouldn't beat yourself up about where you are. You must start to look at how you can change your thinking. When you change your thinking, you change your action; when you change your action, you change your future.

How do you change your thinking? You change what you put in your mind. The mind is the gateway to the heart. You are what you are and you are *where* you are because of what's going into that mind; but you have the ability to change what goes into your mind.

What we put in our mind affects our thinking, our thinking affects our action, and our action affects our future. The major underlying message that's so important is this: acknowledge where you are.

## Acknowledge and Forget

This brings us to the second thing you must do. If someone is responsible for your life's dilemma, then what you ought to do is get rip-roaring, snorting mad about it. I mean, you must get absolutely furious and blame him for everything wrong in your life. Write them a barnburner of a letter. Express every emotion you have and say, "You rascal! You shouldn't'a done this, ya' dirty dog! This was wrong, and I'm furious with you! You made a mess outta' my life, and I'm mad, mad, MAD!" Let it all hang out!

Next, put the letter aside for a few hours. Then get it back out and re-read it to make certain you've included everything. Add a P.S. or two, just in case. Then, take the letter, all ten or twelve pages, go outside, and burn it, page by page. Say to yourself: "I'm gonna forget about it. I'm gonna forgive you for this." Burn the next page. "I forgive you for this." Burn the next page, and say it again. "I forgive you for this."

Let me emphasize a point. When a person experiences serious crimes against them over a long period of time, especially incest, sexual abuse, or physical or verbal abuse, it can be absolutely impossible to forgive without some help. In this case, I encourage you to seek counseling, because forgiveness is absolutely critical. I know it's easy to argue that your perpetrator doesn't deserve for-giveness. I would agree. However, let me encourage you. Allow God to take the decision over for you. Allow God to forgive them. You must forgive them for your *own* benefit.

I do not recommend that you confront this person, particularly at this stage of the game. That can be enormously dangerous. Perhaps you will find closure with them at some later date, provided it doesn't interfere with a recent marriage. Remember not to be vindictive. Hans Selye says the healthiest human emotion is gratitude; the most destructive is revenge. Do not do anything that would hurt another person. Remember that you have forgiven them.

In most cases, to "forget it" is impossible to do. This is because everything we've ever seen, heard, smelled, tasted, touched, or thought has become a part of us. So, when I say "forget it," I mean you must forget you want to take vengeance on them. It's tough to do, but it is so enormously important.

After a lifetime of blaming somebody else for your problems, you can finally forgive them. You are accepting responsibility for your future. This is the most important step you will ever take—accepting that responsibility. From here, you'll discover your life load is so much lighter, that you can move so much faster.

Marcus Aurelius put it this way: "How much more grievous are the consequences of anger than the causes of it?"

I also love what author Bill O'Hearn says. He imagines that in life, you're given only so many pounds or ounces or BTUs of energy, and that every time you love somebody and are nice to somebody, you're given an extra portion of energy. He says that when all the energy is gone, you meet the end of your life. He asks you to imagine that every time you seek revenge or let anger control your life, a double portion of energy is burned. Therefore, you're shortening your own life. Incidentally, medical doctors say exactly the same thing. You need to learn to forgive.

In our society today, we need to not only forgive but also develop a little sense of humor, as well! I love the story of the lady who went in the grocery store and ordered a 25-pound turkey. The butcher said, "We don't have a 25 pounder, but I can get it for you."

She said, "No, I didn't want to buy it. I just wanted to look at it."

He said, "Well, why would you want to look at a 25-pound turkey?"

She said, "I've been on a diet. I've just lost 25 pounds, and I wanted to see what it looked like in one spot." I believe we need to learn to laugh at a lot of things.

In both this bit of forgiveness and in life itself, we need to remember that in the process, the strong and the wise admit they have weaknesses. Now, that's an indication of a healthy self-image. You know, it doesn't bother me that I can't perform an appendectomy. As a matter of fact, there are over 50,000 ways in America to earn a living that I don't know anything about. Why should we get concerned about what we cannot do? Why not concentrate on the things we *can* do? Admit when you have a weakness.

Let me give you some examples. If you had a broken leg, you wouldn't hesitate to go to the doctor to get it fixed. If you have a serious drinking problem, and are further wise and strong, you will admit you cannot handle it. You will seek help of some kind, through AA or any number of other sources. You'll say, "Hey, I got a problem. I can't solve it. Won't you help me?" A lot of times, counseling with a godly counselor will help you forgive the person with whom you're angry if you cannot handle it yourself.

My son Tom and his wife Chachis had been on various eating and exercise programs in the past. Tom needed to lose about 45 pounds. With these diet plans, he'd been on and off, on and off. He went to see Dr. Cooper, who'd been a friend of mine for many years and very helpful to me. After this initial meeting, Tom joined a health club and hired a trainer. Tom needed to lose that weight, while Chachis, on the other hand, needed to *gain* some weight and become stronger. They both hired a trainer.

The first few weeks, they were exhausted. "Ohhhh, I'm so sore!" they would say. But they knew this was going to happen. They had made the commitment. After continued work, Chachis gained the seven pounds, became considerably stronger, and her energy levels dramatically increased. Tom lost over 40 pounds and boosted his energy levels as well. They had a problem and said, "I can't solve it. Won't you help?" A healthy self-image will allow you to do that.

You need to forgive yourself, as well. This, too, might take some counseling. In the cases of sexual abuse or incest, the perpetrator often persuades the victim that it's all his or her fault. Let me give you this assurance: there is nothing on earth you could have done to prevent it. There is nothing you could have done to stop it. If you have any guilty feelings, the perpetrator planted these as the incidents took place. If you cannot forgive yourself, seek some counseling and get your forgiveness.

# The Importance of Self-Image

Let's play a game just for a moment. Let's pretend that one morning, as you're getting ready to go to work, the telephone rings. The voice at the other end says, "Charlie, I hope I didn't wake you up, and I don't wanna slow you down. But I've been thinkin' about you, and I just wanted to call you and tell you how much I admire and respect you. You're the kind of person I enjoy being around. When I'm with you, I'm always encouraged and enthused. You know, Charlie, if there were more people like you, we would have a much better world to live in. Man, if I could spend five minutes a day with you, I'd be able to turn this world upside down. I hope you live a long, happy, and prosperous life so you can encourage other people just as you've encouraged me. That's all I wanted to say, Charlie. Talk to you later."

Here's my question: what kind of day would you have after this? Would it be a pretty good day? If you were a salesperson making sales calls, would you be more enthusiastic, more persuasive, and more committed that day? If you were a physician, would you be a better doctor that day? If you were an attorney, would you be a better attorney?

After that phone call, you'd say: "Why, I'm an asset to my community! I'm a credit to my profession! That ol' boy said so, and he is one smart cookie!"

You wouldn't argue with him. He would have taught you nothing about being a better doctor, a better salesman, or a better lawyer, but you would be better at whatever you do because all of a sudden, the picture you have of yourself, that attitude toward yourself, has changed. When that happens, you create this better self-image, and your performance goes up.

So, how do you change your self-image by yourself—without this phone call? Let's look at some specific steps. Eleanor Roosevelt said many years ago that no one on earth can make you feel inferior without your permission. Nobody. You must first promise yourself that you will never again permit anyone to make you feel less about yourself.

I love the story of this little guy with a pretty intact self-image. The teacher required that the children tell the class about an exciting event that took place over the weekend. The teacher called on little Johnny first and said, "Johnny, what happened to you this weekend?"

Johnny said, "Aw, teacher, it was wonderful! My dad took me fishin', and we caught 75 catfish. Each one of them weighed 75 pounds."

The teacher said, "Now, Johnny! You know that could not possibly be true!"

Johnny answered back, "Oh, yes, it is!"

"Now, Johnny, I know it cannot be the truth. Why, what would you think if I said that on the way to school this morning, I was confronted by a thousand-pound grizzly bear about to jump on me and eat me up? What's more, a little bitty dog, weighing about three pounds, came up, jumped, and grabbed the grizzly bear by the nose. He threw it down and shook him until he killed the bear. What would you think about that? Would you believe it?"

Johnny smiled. "Yes, ma'am, I sure would! As a matter of fact, that was my dog!"

I would say that little Johnny's self-image was pretty okay.

How does your image affect your performance? And how does the way you see other people affect their performance?

Remember: "If you do not see yourself as a winner, you cannot perform as a winner."

When our daughter, Julie, was in the fifth grade, the teacher came to us and said, "Julie is an average student. She'll make C's primarily, the occasional B, and the occasional D. But don't worry about it. She's very personable. She makes a lot of friends. But don't be too hard on her if she's not a top performer." We never told our little girl she was a C-student; the teacher never told our little girl she was a C-student. But I'm certain in a thousand different ways we communicated to Julie that we expected a C-performance out of her.

Three years ago, after being out of school for something like 17 years, Julie went back to school. During her first semester, she carried 16 very tough hours, including two very difficult labs. She made the Dean's List and came within a whisper of a 4.0. One night, I called her house to talk to her and her husband, Jim Norman, who was the CEO of our company, picked up. I said, "Lemme speak to Julie," after I had chatted with Jim.

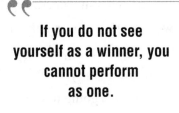

**If you do not see yourself as a winner, you cannot perform as one.**

Jim started laughing. "Julie's next door teaching Diane advanced math."

Jim was laughing because all of her life, Julie had said that old refrain seventeen thousand times, "Well, you know, I just can't learn math." But there she was over there, *teaching* advanced math to one of the neighbors.

What, exactly, had happened? Well, she explained it to me. "Dad, I discovered that knowledge reveals itself to anyone who diligently pursues it. I had never really mastered the formulas. When I learned those formulas, I thought—math is a snap! It is easy!"

Is this an unusual story? How many of you, ten or more years after you got out of your formal education, decided to go back for more education? How many of you, when you went back, did better—and in some cases *substantially* better—than you did when you'd been in school the first time?

When you went back, you planned to do better. You prepared to do better. You expected to do better, and you went back at your own expense. You had something different called commitment. Let me tell you something else. Over the years, you learned you were a bright, productive person. That good self-image picture you created alongside your ambition to go back really said an awful lot about you. When the image changes, the performance absolutely is going to change.

# The Influence of Crowds

Before we dive into crowd talk, you must understand the following: "Some of us learn from other people's mistakes, and the rest of us have to be other people."

The *LA Times* once printed a substantial study about enormously successful people. At one stage of their lives, these successful people made a deliberate choice to associate with different crowds. Why is this important? Growing up, I'm sure you heard the excuse—spoken about someone in trouble— "He just got mixed up in the wrong crowd." I'll bet every one of us has! There's a connection between the crowd and what you do in life.

Unfortunately, we have an entirely different crowd today. This influential crowd is better known as an "income suppressant." Many people refer to this as "television." Think about the crowd you run with when you look at television: people who commit murders, drive-by shootings, violence, rapes, racist acts, and sexist acts. You see absolutely everything. When you associate with these people, you influence yourself. When Mom and Dad sit and watch it with their children, they're tacitly saying it's okay to cuss, it's okay to be violent, and it's okay to get drunk. These parents actually encourage participation by watching it.

The tragedy is that television could be so enormously helpful. The dramatization could be powerful and beneficial. Everything you see around you and on television goes into your mind and affects your thinking. Your thinking affects your performance.

Your performance affects the image of yourself that you hold in your head.

To improve your image of yourself, it's essential that you improve your memory. How many times have you bragged about having a lousy memory? When you tell yourself and other people, "Oh, I can remember faces, but I cannot remember names!" over and over, you become like my daughter and her math. Your inability to remember becomes a reality.

I don't necessarily believe people must remember three hundred people right after they meet them. However, let me give you a little story. We teach a three-day seminar called Born to Win. Several years ago, we were discussing memory in that seminar. A man named Dan Clark and his wife, Kelly, from Salt Lake City, attended. He was an All-American football player, a big defensive end, a good-looking guy, and an outstanding speaker. She was the beauty queen: an absolutely gorgeous, wonderfully personable, sweet individual.

We had 100 people at the seminar. The memory teacher that day was giving out points: two points if you got the first and last name of every person there. Kelly was the first one up. She only missed one out of a possible two hundred. When Kelly stepped up to receive her award, she broke down and wept. "All of my life, I thought I was dumb. I just learned in the last hour and a half that I'm a very bright person."

This story has a double point. There are a lot of good memory books and techniques that can work to improve your image. These techniques give you added confidence. What I'm really talking about here is growth. Every time you take a step forward, every time you learn something of value, you work to improve that picture.

You need to keep growing. Terry Bradshaw says, "The life of a winner is the result of an unswerving commitment to a never-ending process of self-completion."

People ask my staff and my family the same question all the time. "Is Zig really up like that all the time?"

Let me tell you, folks, I am up. But there is a difference between being "up" and being "on." If you're *on* 100% of the time, you're on something that's going to kill you.

The only time I get "down" is when I am physically exhausted. Years ago, I learned not to make important decisions when I'm physically exhausted. When I finish a three or four-hour seminar, for example, I'm exhausted. My wife, "the redhead," has lunch for me. We'll eat and visit for about an hour. Then, I will take a nap for about 30 or 40 minutes. When I get up, I will take a casual walk for about 30 minutes, and then I'll take a fast walk for about 30 minutes. I'll be ready to go again. This is how I stay "up" an overwhelming majority of the time.

Furthermore, I practice what I preach. I read three hours a day, just as I have for twenty years. Now, that is a lot of input.

As I work through this discussion, I listen to myself more carefully than anybody here. This is my self-talk. When I say to you, "This is what you ought to do," I'm actually saying to myself. "Yeah, Ziglar! That sounds like a good idea, man! Do it yourself!"

You know what? I do exactly what I am saying to you, to the very best of my ability.

## Steps to Build a Self-Image

How do you build a self-image? First of all, it's essential to remember that failure is an event. Failure is not a person. For example, a musician hits a sour note. Does that mean he's a failure as a musician? A student misses a question. Does that mean she's a failure as a student? The cook burns the beans. Does that mean he's a failure as a cook? Failure is an event; it is not a person. Yesterday ended last night; today is a brand-new day. It's yours!

I love the story told of the 37-year-old scrubwoman on welfare. To quote her, she had been born ugly, and then somebody had scared her. As she pondered her welfare and her scrub-floor job, she started doing a little personal evaluation. She picked up a book entitled *The Magic of Believing*. Now, note that I do believe in the magic of believing! But I do not believe in magic.

The scrubwoman read this particular book. It gave her a new picture of herself; it gave her new hope. Remember: "If there's hope in the future, there is power in the present." She remembered that when she had been in school, she had had the ability to make people laugh. She decided she would start practicing again on her friends. She started making people laugh once more at social functions. Later, and for a number of years, in fact, Phyllis Diller earned over a million dollars a year making people laugh.

Incidentally, if you saw her at 37 and also saw her at 65, you would know she was a more attractive person at 65 than she was at 37. I'm here to tell you, we can change; we can grow. We can become more than we are. If you don't like who you are and where you are, don't sweat it. You're not stuck.

## Take a Self-Inventory

The next step is to take inventory of yourself. Remember that: "You can't climb the ladder of success dressed in the costume of failure."

> If there's hope in the future, there is power in the present.

Let's start with this question: how much inventory would you state for your health? You might remember a man named Barney Clark, who was given a mechanical heart implant. The implant cost several million dollars and extended his life only a few weeks. You've got a good heart. If that mechanical one was worth several million dollars, how much is yours worth? Let's push this further. I read about a lady who went to a doctor about a rash on her face. He prescribed some drugs. The drugs settled in her eyes, and she lost her sight. The insurance company gave her a check for a million dollars. What would you take for yours?

I read about a lady who was injured in an airplane accident who lost her ability to walk. They gave her a million dollars. What would you take for your legs? How many of you recognize the name, Betty Grable? What do you remember about Betty Grable? Legs, right?

She had a beautiful face and nice arms, but we always remember her legs. Those legs were insured for a million dollars. How much would you take for yours? Notice that when you begin to evaluate yourself, the numbers get really high. When you take inventory, you start to realize you really are extraordinarily well off.

Let me remind you of my friend, John Foppe. He was born without any arms. John Foppe said to me, "You know, Zig, I can only do so much with no arms. But my mind is what I can do so many things with."

If you had a $50,000 automobile and somebody said something ugly about it, you would get upset. "What do you mean, talkin' about this $50,000 car? Man, it's magnificent!" Now, you're allowed to say something ugly about it, of course, but nobody else is allowed.

What about the billion-dollar *you*? You were fearfully and wonderfully made. Evaluate yourself. I'm not talking about a super-inflated, "I am the greatest" ego. I'm talking about a simple, healthy self-acceptance.

To improve your self-image, you need to make up, dress up, and "go up." Saturday is now one of the best days around my house. The Redhead makes this trip, generally, every Saturday we're in town. She's gone about two hours, and when she comes back, she's stepping just a little bit higher. She's smiling a little bit more broadly; she's a little friendlier. The Redhead has been to the beauty shop. I've never been able to figure out why rearranging a few hairs on the head changes everything. But don't you feel more competent and more confident when you're sharp-looking? They've proven over and over that picture days at school create well-behaved kids who actually perform better throughout the day. When you look sharp, you feel sharp; that, in turn, makes you sharp. When you make up and dress up, your chances of "going up" are absolutely better.

Do you remember Li'l Abner? I used to love Li'l Abner. My favorite character was Bull Moose. Bull Moose used to say, "If it's good for Bull Moose, it's good for the world." That's the kind of guy who had a good, healthy self-image. Unfortunately, of course, his went into egotism.

They used to have a Sadie Hawkins Day in a lot of the southern schools. At Sadie Hawkins Day, everybody dressed up in raggedy clothes. They stopped having them after two or three years. That's because they created violence, vandalism, poor conduct, and poor performance.

When you make up and dress up, your chances of "going up" in your performance and self-image are definitely improved.

You need to get the bear out of the trap. What do I mean by this? Over in Keithville, Louisiana, they had an incredible amount of excitement. Late one Saturday afternoon, just as it was getting dark, somebody rode through a little underbrush area. They looked up in the tree to see a black bear. They notified everybody——the fire department, the police, a veterinarian, and everyone from the town. They decided to let the veterinarian start shooting the bear with tranquilizer darts. The fire department held out a net to catch him when he fell out.

They kept shooting that sucker, and he kept staying up there. They finally decided they'd patiently wait all night. They posted a lookout to see if any activity took place up there, but nothing happened. The next morning, they still couldn't get him out. They decided they were going to have to cut the tree down because they didn't want the black bear running loose in the neighborhood. When they cut the tree down, they were prepared to do what they needed to do to make certain he didn't get hurt or hurt anybody else. When the tree came down, they discovered the bear was actually a plastic bag filled with garbage.

So many people around the world have a "bear in the tree." They've got their past buried in their mind. They concentrate on the negatives of life, and as a result, they never really end up doing all the things they're capable of doing.

Your self-image is enormously important on your road to success.

# 2

# WHAT YOU PUT
# IN YOUR BRAIN

There was this fellow driving in a "non-professional" manner—
let's put it that way. A police officer arrested him and took him
to night court. As the man stood before the presiding judge, the
judge said, "Now, I want you to do a few things."

The fellow said, "Like what?"

"I want you to lift your hands straight up over your head."

The fellow said, "I can't do that."

"Why can't you?"

He said, "I was injured in a skiing accident."

"Okay," the judge said. "I want you to turn your head left to right."

"I can't do that."

"Why?"

"I was injured in a diving accident," the man explained.

The judge said, "I want you to bend over and touch your toes."

"I can't do that," the man said.

"How come you can't?" the judge asked.

"I injured my back liftin'."

"All right. I want you to stand on one leg."

But he said, "I can't do that."

"Why?" the judge asked for a final time.

"Cause I'm drunk."

The judge said, "All right. That'll be $1,000 or 90 days. Which will you choose?"

He said, "I'll take the $1,000!"

Now, I would say this fellow had a great presence of mind!

## The Image Problem

Remember the following: "If you don't see yourself as a winner, then you cannot perform as a winner."

What causes a good majority of the image problems we have? Why is it that over 90% of the acknowledged beauties of the Hollywood world, the envies of so many average people, want to change the way they are? To put it simply: they have a false perception of their image. The beauty magazines, the fashion magazines, and the articles we read are constantly lauding beauty, health, and brains. And these things, obviously, could be considered assets. Or, they could be liabilities. Unfortunately, we are not putting enough emphasis on the things that really make a difference: character qualities.

The input into our brains is overwhelmingly negative. Dr. Shad Helmstetter says that the typical 16-year-old has been told 147,000 times that he "can't do it." If you tell a youngster 147,000 times he can't do something, he is likely to believe it. A lot of parents say things like:

"You never do anything right!"
"You're always late!"
"That's dumb."
"You can't learn math!"

Well, think of the pictures those statements make in the mind of the person.

I'm convinced that the greatest damage the black man has endured from the white man has been on his self-image. Now, I'm a child of the South. I was raised in Mississippi. When I was a boy, I used to go to the Shirley Temple movies. Yes: Shirley Temple and I really are around the same age. I thought those movies were so cute. She was always dancing and singing songs, like "Little Miss Lollipop," or "On the Good Ship Lollipop." She was just "Little Miss Perfect!"

I vividly remember seeing this movie, but, until Bill Cosby explained it to me through the eyes of a black person, I had no idea—it just never registered with me—the incredible damage that had been done. In this movie, there was a birthday party. Little Miss Shirley was five years old. She had her friends around, and they were having their cake and ice cream. The party was just about over when this little African-American girl, who was tall and slender, about thirteen or fourteen years old, with two much younger friends, came up to Miss Shirley. "Miss Shirley," she said, "we brought you a present." Take a minute to really understand that picture—a thirteen-year-old addressing a five-year-old in this manner.

Miss Shirley said, "Ohhh, thank you very much! Now, you can have some of our leftover birthday cake." The little black girl put her hands over her eyes and said, "Oh, Miss Shirley!" Can you see what this scene would do to the self-image of a black man?

Now, when I originally watched it as a child, I just thought it was cute. That was one of the greatest eye-opening experiences I have ever had.

Let me give you a couple of examples of what happens when we look at people properly.

This story appeared in *Reader's Digest* quite a few years ago. A balloon salesman was on the streets of New York selling balloons. Every time he saw his crowd was growing smaller, he released a balloon—maybe a white one. People would watch those things go up and then gather around and buy again. In a few minutes, he would release a red one, and the same thing would happen. Then, he would release a yellow one.

After a while, a little African-American youngster walked up and tugged on his sleeve. He said, "Mister, if you were to release one of the black ones, would it go up?"

With the wisdom you really would not expect to find in someone who was selling balloons on the street, the balloon salesman looked down at the youngster and said, "Son, it's what's inside of those balloons that make them go up."

That's what we need to understand. It's what's inside that's going to make us successful. As my psychologist friend Don Beck says, we are all packaged a little differently. On the inside, the heart and the mind are all exactly the same color.

One of the most comprehensive articles I've ever read was in the February 1992 issue of *Scientific American*. It speaks of over five hundred Indonesian immigrant students in America. They had been in detention camps for two or three years, and their educational processes had been hampered. Suddenly, they found themselves in the inner cities of America. The researchers discovered some interesting things. Number one: the students with larger families had better grades. That's fascinating because the older students in the family were teaching the younger kids. Secondly, they discovered that when the parents read to the students, whether it was in their native tongue or in English, their grades were absolutely fabulous. They found that when the parents reinforced their culture and heritage, the students' grades were affected as a direct result. They discovered that when the parents and the teachers worked together, the results were absolutely magnificent.

In the article, they also discussed the post-World War II Japanese prejudice. They noted that the Japanese students who were given similar heritage-based treatment at home alongside teacher cooperation had the same results. They did a study of African Americans in Chicago and discovered exactly the same thing. The Jewish people lent the same discovery. It doesn't make any difference which continent you're from; it doesn't make any difference what color your skin is. When these people got the same treatment, they produced the same results.

Let's think together. If everyone knew that treatment altered self-image—treatment at home and treatment at school—would everything change? How you treat people has a bearing on their self-image. Their image has a direct bearing on their performance.

Let me give you a classic, tragic example of what happens when a youngster has a poor self-image and is rejected.

In March 1993, a fourteen-year-old killed a policeman and seriously wounded three of his neighbors. Through the exchange of gunfire, the child was also killed. Incredibly, his father was on the police force. Well, what caused these events? His classmates called him a "nerd." They made fun of his clothing. He did poorly in school. His parents disciplined him; they made him stay at home that Saturday to study. Something "snapped." He *reacted* to what had happened with tragic results.

What would have happened in that child's life had even one student come to him and said, "I think you're a neat guy. I'd like to be your friend." I'm not saying this to even mildly hint at putting guilt on any of his classmates. You can't saw sawdust; you can't undo what has already happened. We can learn from this and prepare for the future. Had his self-image been different, he would have been a different person. He had been conditioned to believe he was a failure. Negative conditioning is the mother of learning, the father of action, and the architect of failure. Positive conditioning is the mother of learning, the father of action, and the architect of success.

Do you respond to life, or do you react to life? About five years ago, I was in San Francisco, California, doing a seminar. I wasn't far from Los Gatos, California, and I attended a football practice session at Los Gatos High School. The coach was Charlie Wedemeyer, and the practice session was fascinating. Charlie and I spent about an hour and a half together, just talking. Every three minutes, one of the assistant coaches would come running up to say, "Charlie, they're trap blockin' us every time on that play! What do we do?" Immediately, Charlie would give him an answer. A few minutes later, an assistant coach would come back to him and say, "Charlie, that guy's beatin' us around the end every time. What can we do?" Charlie would give an answer. He had been watching and listening intently. He led his team to the only state championship they have ever won.

The fascinating thing here is that Charlie Wedemeyer cannot "talk" as you and I know of talking. As a matter of fact, he has Lou Gehrig's disease. The only parts of his body that will even move are his eyelids and his mouth. His vocal cords are paralyzed; nothing comes out. Only his lips move. His wife, Lucy, reads his lips and communicates the messages.

I've never seen anybody with a healthier self-image. In the seventies, Charlie was Hawaii's athlete of the decade. He was a superb physical specimen in every way before he fell victim to the disease. He understands that his value is not wrapped up in what he can do physically.

He's an inspiration. He has one of the greatest senses of humor. He even travels a lot, despite the fact that it's a difficult thing to haul the equipment, take the nurse, and take his wife everywhere. He goes frequently to address high schools and prisons. He makes the statement, and then Lucy repeats it. In 1992, he was honored as the Disabled American of the Year. Former President Bush was supposed to attend, but, at the last minute, he had to cancel. When Charlie made his speech, with Lucy doing all the talking, he said he hated that the president couldn't be there, because he was going to say to him, "Read my lips." He had responded to what had happened to him, rather than reacted.

## Improper Brain Input

How many of you honestly believe the works of Billy Graham, Abraham Lincoln, Helen Keller, Martin Luther King, Jr., Moses, Confucius, Mahatma Gandhi, and Jesus Christ have had a positive influence on both America and the world? How many of you believe that the input of Prince, Madonna, 2 Live Crew, or Ice-T could have negatively influenced our behavior in America? Do you remember Madonna's "sex books"? I think seven or eight hundred thousand copies were sold very quickly at fifty bucks a throw. Time Warner only put two restrictions on the books: they stated she could not have sex with a religious object in the pictures, and she could not have sex with an animal.

Will this build the kind of America that can solve its four trillion-dollar deficit? Will this build the kind of America that will solve our crime problem, bring our families back together, and make our streets safe? Remember that, "Building a better you is the first step to building a better America." Is what you learn from the media building a better you?

> **Building a better you is the first step to building a better America.**

If good input produces good results, then we cannot deny the fact that improper input will produce improper and undesirable results. Aren't we influenced by what we see?

Let me give you one of the great truths of life: people you talk to might not believe everything you say, but I can guarantee you those people are going to believe everything you *do*. Does any input from your life influence your output?

Be careful about what you put in your mind. Suppose you were told, "You're a winner!" or, "You're a marvelous human being, and here's why!" over and over again. Would this have a positive influence on you? Suppose you were told over and over, "You're a dummy!" or, "You can't do it!" Do you think this could have a negative influence on your life?

In the *Dallas Morning News* on March 10th, 1993, they printed a substantial article about damaged self-images as a result of comparison to the "glamour" people and the "brains" of the world. Do we consider that to constitute success?

You'll probably be surprised to learn that there are infinitely more millionaire salespeople than millionaire doctors. You'll probably be amazed to learn that there are more millionaires in America with average jobs. As a matter of fact, according to *US*

*News and World Report,* less than one percent of all American millionaires are in athletics, entertainment, music, television, and the movies combined. Less than one percent! The other ninety-nine percent are people like you and me who hung in there over a long period of time. We need to get a different picture of ourselves.

What causes poor self-image? Well, for one, poverty can be a cause of poor self-image. For example, if a home is unsafe, making a child unwilling to bring his friends there, the child is impacted. This could be because of a parent who is addicted to alcohol or substances, or a whole host of other reasons. The child could be embarrassed to introduce people to them; as a result, the child could create a poor self-image of himself and his family. Harsh treatment, physical abuse, and verbal abuse can all have an impact as well.

However, the number one cause of a poor self-image is a lack of unconditional love. Unconditional love occurs when you accept and love your child not because he's an A student, not because he cleans his room, not because he's home on time, but because he is yours. You unconditionally accept your child as yours.

One of the most destructive things to a self-image occurs with incest or sexual abuse. When a single mother with a little girl invites her boyfriend to come live with her, it's probable she's just extended an invitation to the neighborhood pedophile. The records are crystal clear: the odds of a pedophile attempting to date the neighborhood single mother go up dramatically. It happens too many times for it to be a coincidence.

## Manifestations of a Poor Self-Image

Have you ever noticed the way the media treats two-parent families, or the way it deals with Catholics and Protestants, people with religious convictions and persuasions? When was the last time you saw a television series with a regular husband and wife who were the heroes of the series? Most of the time, the father is either brutal or a wimp. Too much of the time, the children make ol' Dad look like an idiot; they appear smarter than both Mom and Dad put together. This media presentation creates a real problem.

It pains me to say this, but negative preachers are one of the biggest causes of a poor self-image. All they talk about is what "God's gonna do to ya'!" These preachers only want to talk about hell and brimstone. Now don't misunderstand: I think some of that ought to be there. I heard somebody say once that if there were more "hell" in the pulpit, there'd be less of it in the streets! However, let me simply say we need to look at the positive side, as well.

I want to emphasize that when you explore the manifestations of poor self-image, it will help us to identify the people we're dealing with and, hopefully, ourselves. If we can tell that person has the same problem that we do, then we're in a position to offer a solution.

An example of these manifestations lies with this: jealousy without cause. I've heard a husband or wife say so many times, "Oh, I just love him so much, I can't let him out of my sight!" What she's really saying is, "I cannot believe he or she would be faithful to me. Poor li'l ol' me!"

Another manifestation of low self-image is failing to give your best effort. See, if you don't give your best effort, you can always shrug and say, "Had I really tried, I would have succeeded." Had you tried and failed, however, you might have deteriorated your self-image even more.

These poor self-image people don't finish their projects. Whether their project is cutting the grass or getting the report in on time, they don't finish it. When you finish, you get recognition; you get praise. When you believe you don't deserve praise, you don't finish. These people don't sit there and think this through, but this is what happens instinctively.

These people often think others are laughing at them. They have a tendency to quiz a group after they've broken up, asking, "What were y'all talkin' about? Didja mention me?" They're overly sensitive to criticism.

They also can't handle a compliment: "Boy, this is one of the most delicious casseroles I've ever eaten!"

"I wish I'd had time to marinate the veal a little bit longer," the low self-image person says.

> When you finish, you get recognition; you get praise. When you believe you don't deserve praise, you don't finish.

Or it could go something like this: "My, that's a beautiful dress you've got on!"

"Well, I've been wearing it for three years, but thank you," they reply.

Or this: "My, your house is always so neat!"

"Well, I wish I'd had more time to take care of some of the panels."

They just cannot say, "Thank you" and accept these simple compliments, which shows a sign of a good, healthy self-image. This sort of person insists on picking up the check. You go out with somebody for coffee or a meal, and, even though they cannot afford it, say, "Lemme pick up the check." They feel that they are not worthy of your company unless they are giving you something—so they pick up the check.

They dress in revealing clothes. Fishermen call this "trolling." The only problem with trolling is that sometimes you pick up an old boot or a stump, and you find out it's tougher to get them off the hook than it was to get them on.

If this low self-esteem person is a salesperson, he fails to ask for the order. I was in direct sales for fifteen years. I've seen hundreds of efforts to close the sale. The salesperson talks and talks, and he never asks for the order. Finally, the prospect says, "Well, John, you're not tryin' to sell me somethin', are ya'?"

"Oh, no! No, no!" the salesperson says.

You've got to remember the following statement: "Selling is essentially a transfer of feelings." Was this salesperson transferring his feelings of happiness with himself? With his self-image?

My question to these people is: well, what are you? A professional visitor? We've discovered that sales escalate dramatically with greater salesperson self-image. If you have the right image, you're selling the right product; if you feel good about yourself and what you're selling, you want the other person to own it for *their* benefit—not yours!

Furthermore, these poor self-image people continually over-promise. We've all seen it. Every new coach or manager over-promises fast results. Politicians are notoriously famous for this, are they not? They over-promise because they are afraid they won't be accepted unless they promise the right things.

Old "Motor-Mouth" is one of the signs of a low self-image, as well. These people talk all the time. They can't slow down because they feel they've always got to be selling. We've all experienced a Motor-Mouth. You head to Motor-Mouth's house for a short visit, and you're blocked from leaving. He stands in the way; he has something else to tell you. Always, there's something else to tell you. He opens the door of your car for you, and as you're backing out, he says, "Roll down the window! One more thing to tell ya!" Old Motor-Mouth has a poor self-image.

On the other hand, sometimes a silent mouth is a sign of poor self-image as well. They are simply of the belief that what they have to say is of very little value; consequently, they do not say anything.

Of course, a filthy mouth is one of the surest giveaways of a low self-image. They think they must punctuate everything they say to force people to listen to them.

Bob Hope said if you eliminated the filth from our movies today, we'd be back to silent film. I think he is really close to being right. I believe it was Ann Landers who did a study that found that roughly ninety-nine percent of American people believe that

TV and movies play down to us. We're actually offended by a lot of the language. So, what can we do about it? Don't go!

The "class clown" is, in so many cases, simply an individual with a poor self-image as well.

In fact, so many things can be signs of a poor self-image, you can even include a golf ball! I found one when I was out walking. Interestingly enough, it was out of bounds. It was a brand-new Titleist. On it was written the words "Strike Three." Does that tell you something? Does that say to you, "I'm a lousy golfer, and I'm gonna foul it up! I'm gonna strike out again!" These are all signs of a low self-image.

Let's translate these poor self-image manifestations into other professions and areas of life.

The student with a poor self-image, for example, would never confront the teacher over a grade, even when he knows he deserves a better one. He wouldn't ask the pretty girl for a date because, in his mind, she doesn't "go" with him and he doesn't "deserve" her. The tragedy is she probably wanted to go out with him!

The office worker with a self-image problem would never assert herself and ask for a raise, even when she knows the caliber of her work warrants more pay. If she doesn't get the raise and recognition she deserves, she will become resentful and feel that no one understands and appreciates her. The net result is a negative effect on her performance and a reduction in the possibility of a future raise.

The husband or wife with a poor self-image becomes a doormat for his or her spouse. This low self-image spouse never voices his own opinions; he or she never asks the spouse to look at the other side or explore what they may think. This doesn't make for a good relationship.

## Pleasing Everyone: Self-Image Syndrome

There's evidence that "good ol' Joe," just the guy down the street, and his distaff counterpart actually have a common problem, one that has nothing to do with age, sex, education, size, or skin color. He has an "I must be a nice guy and never offend anyone" self-image syndrome. As a youngster, he smoked cigarettes he didn't want, took the drink he didn't like, laughed at dirty jokes that actually offended him, joined the gang he secretly disliked, and went along with conduct he secretly abhorred.

About a month ago, *USA TODAY* printed an article about drinking at colleges. They said a lot of people who get drunk do so because they think everybody expects them to. They want to be accepted. The survey proved that these drinkers fail in both their own self-image and in the estimation of others. They're pursuing a false idea.

These please-everyone people are inclined to marry their first romantic interest. The fear of not being accepted by anyone else frequently leads these people to foolish and impetuous behavior, including early marriage or promiscuous behavior. As an adult, this person has a tendency to tell people what he or she thinks they want to hear. For example, they would never send an overcooked steak back to the kitchen. They let others take their parking spot and don't object when a co-worker takes credit for work they have done.

There once was a lady who was driving a big, luxury automobile. She was headed for a parking spot in this big, crowded parking lot. Suddenly, a young guy with a bitty sports car zipped right in front of her, taking her spot. He hopped out and waved at her, saying, "When you're young and strong and athletic, you can do things like this!" She didn't say a word. She backed her car up and then charged right into his, smashing it! Then, she backed up and hit it again.

The young man came running back. He said, "What on earth are you doin'?"

She said, "I'm doin' what I wanna do; you can do that when you're old and rich."

There was nothing wrong with her self-image; she had had enough!

## Building Your Self-Image

Understand this: if your self-image is healthy, you can conduct yourself in this manner. You can do what you want, and what you do will be good. However, if you do things just to gain acceptance, you're gaining everything *but* acceptance. The reason is simple: you're not presenting the real you. In fact, you're presenting a phony. Most people, including other phonies, don't like a phony.

Building a healthy self-image needs to be more than just what we must do as individuals. We need to do something about it on a national level. No snowflake ever blames itself for the blizzard. No raindrop ever blames itself for the flood. But each one of us has a responsibility to our country and to our society.

I want to emphasize a point. I believe I am a very pragmatic individual. In this morning's little funny, ol' Dennis the Menace said, "I don't bite my fingernails! I know where they've been!" Now you see, Dennis was being pragmatic. I want to be pragmatic as I look at the following causes of poor self-image and what we can do about it.

At the time of this writing, news has been flooded with the following fact: boys continually sexually harass girls starting in fifth grade, all the way through high school and college. Eighty percent of these girls complained about hearing lewd remarks, being patted and pinched, and having obscene gestures made at them. The most common thing these girls said was that they felt dirty, that these events injured their self-esteem.

That's why I was so stunned when I picked up the paper yesterday. In the March 28th, 1993 *Dallas Morning News,* Judge Frank Thornton said that you could not teach a sex education course in school while using the words "spirituality," "soul," or "moral." You cannot even use those words! One court ruled last week that the word "abstinence" was not allowed in a sex education course, saying the word is a "religious" teaching.

Let me emphasize a point. I believe in things that work. If what they're doing worked, I would tuck my tail between my legs and never say another word about it. But what they're teaching is not working.

In the schools in which they teach sex education, 113 girls out of 1,000 become pregnant. According to Focus on the Family, the schools in which they teach moral values and abstinence have 3 pregnancies out of 1,000. I'm a taxpayer, just like you, and I have to support the result of all of those pregnancies.

Let me say it again: via one method, 113 out of 1,000 end up pregnant; via the other, 3 out of 1,000 end up pregnant.

Elayne Bennett, the wife of Bill Bennett, our former secretary of education and drug czar, has a program in inner-city Washington, D.C., called "Friends." She teaches working together, abstinence, and moral values. In the last three years, there hasn't been a single pregnancy among those who take the course. Now, there's such a fear of anything "religious" in our schools. Note that the Constitution does not separate us from religion. We have freedom *of* religion, of course; but we do not have freedom *from* religion.

A *Wall Street Journal* survey shows that eighty-four percent of Americans would like their children to be taught values. The reason is that in 1776, three million Americans produced Thomas Jefferson, George Washington, Benjamin Franklin, Alexander Hamilton, John Adams, Monroe—you name 'em! Right across the board. In 1993, two hundred and fifty million Americans produced—fill in the blanks.

What were they taught in 1776? According to the Thomas Jefferson Research Institute, over ninety percent of it was of a moral, ethical, or religious nature.

I love what Ann Melvin of the *Dallas Morning News* said: "Something is wrong when we can teach a child to use a condom before recess but won't let them pray before lunch."

# The Importance of Moral Values

Please understand, I'm not on a roll to get religion back in the schools. I am on a roll to get *moral values* back in the schools.

According to psychiatrist Robert Coles of Harvard University, "Many school teachers are afraid to bring up moral and spiritual questions for fear that they violate the Constitution. It's a tragedy intellectually as well as morally and spiritually. This might relate to the educational problems among some children. A large number of the schools' assumptions are materialistic and agnostic. There's a cultural conflict between families and schools. That conflict may have some bearing on what children learn and what they don't learn, and how children behave in school."

Why are my feelings so strong on this? For 15 years, we've had a course for both children and adults called "I CAN." We don't delve into religion, but we do teach honesty, character, integrity, hard work, enthusiasm, responsibility, and commitment. What is the result? Grades are better. Attendance is up, drug use is down, and attitudes are better. There is less violence and less vandalism.

Indianapolis, Indiana native Charlie Pfluger came to one of our seminars on "I CAN." He was assistant principal at an inner-city school in Indianapolis that was about to close. After the seminar, he went back with more ideas and more excitement than he could use. He took a silver dollar, put it on a piece of cardboard, and drew it for a cutout. On one side, he put "PLA" for "Positive Life Attitude," and on the other side, he put "I CAN."

They started giving the kids an "I CAN dollar" every time they did something a little unusual. If they helped an old lady across the street, if they picked up trash on the school grounds without being told, if they erased the blackboard, if they graciously and enthusiastically welcomed a newcomer to school, the kids would receive an "I CAN dollar." When they accumulated a hundred of them, the kids would receive a "Winner's" T-shirt.

There were 593 kids at Charlie's school. Normally, when you're about to close a school, nobody cares what happens in the school. Proving this point wrong, 587 of those kids won those "Winner" T-shirts! Charlie said it got to be hilarious. When a piece of paper blew across the schoolyard, nine kids ran it down. Their blackboards were cleaner than ever. Old ladies who didn't want to cross the street had to cross the street, anyway! When a newcomer came to the school, about 75 of the kids welcomed him.

Most importantly, during that time, not a single act of violence, not a single act of vandalism, and not a single drug arrest occurred. Grades were better for the first time because the kids were required to go home and thank their parents for something nice they did that day. Parents, teachers, and kids became a unit. During that "I CAN" class, those children were taught respect, courtesy, enthusiasm, hard work, and discipline. Those are the values we're talking about.

For many years, it's been a tragedy that we have been too intimidated to talk about religion and politics. I challenge you to think of any two subjects more important than religion and politics. The fact that we haven't gotten involved in politics is the reason our country is in the turmoil it is today. Even Norman Lear, who leans so far left he has to clench his fingers from dragging them on the ground, said, "We have gone too far. We've got to put some of these values back in our schools."

How important are moral values? How many of you think honesty is a moral value? According to the Chamber of Commerce, fifty to sixty percent of all businesses go bankrupt because of employee theft. In the last ten years, 85% of all new jobs have been created by businesses of 50 people or less. Put those numbers together. How many tens of thousands of people are out of work today because they were not taught moral values, either by their parents or by the educational system?

I believe that every person who has been a victim of rape, mugging, or a drive-by shooting, if you were to ask them, would say, "Man alive, I wish that person had been taught some moral values." We all probably remember the Fort Worth fiasco, in which Donald Thomas was senselessly shot and killed by three skinheads because he was black. I'll guarantee you that Carolyn Thomas wishes there were more moral values in school. On television, she is a beautiful lady who responded instead of reacting. Was she hurting? Of course, she was. She understood, though, that hate and vengeance would not solve the problem. She explained, "What we need and want is peace and justice."

## Something Bigger than Ourselves

Mary Crowley has been a friend and hero of mine over the last 20 years. Mary Crowley said to me many years ago: "Zig, there comes a time in everybody's life when they encounter problems they cannot solve. That's when something greater than we are needs to take over."

If you've ever participated in Alcoholics Anonymous or any of the other 12-step programs, you know the two keys to success. The first key is to acknowledge you cannot handle the problem; you need help from a "higher power," or God as you understand Him. The second key to staying sober is to help somebody *else* stay sober. Is accepting responsibility for your brother a moral value? I believe so.

Six years ago, I was in Atlanta, Georgia, doing a seminar. When it was over, a lady seated in the second row with her husband came up. She said, "Mr. Ziglar, I'm Janet McBarron; I'm the one who wrote you the letter."

I said, "Yes, Janet. It's an absolute delight to see you."

"I just wanted to elaborate. Like you, I weighed well over 200 pounds for a number of years. As you can clearly see, I'm no longer overweight. Unlike you, I used to smoke two to three packs of cigarettes a day. I no longer smoke. Unlike you, I used to drink, and I'm embarrassed to say that on one or two occasions, I drank too much. I no longer drink. Mr. Ziglar, my self-image was at rock bottom. It was down to zero. I started listening to you over and over.

"I heard you quote Dr. Joyce Brothers, who said, 'You cannot consistently perform in a manner which is inconsistent with the way you see yourself.' I especially appreciated the fact you kept emphasizing that life is tough, but when you're tough on yourself, life is gonna be infinitely easier on you. I love that you kept saying, 'If you don't like who you are and where you are, don't worry about it: you're not stuck. You can grow; you can change.' Mr. Ziglar, let me re-introduce myself. I'm Janet McBarron, M.D. I worked my way through medical school as a full-time nurse. I'm one of five women in America who specializes in bariatrics, weight management, and weight control."

With the right input, she made a commitment. She put in a lot of hard work, and she had a willingness to serve. She wanted to be happy, and she is. Let me tell you one of the reasons she is happy. She is happy because she is working and helping everyone else. Today, Janet McBarron is a published author. She has three clinics. Over 500,000 of her books have been sold. Most notably, she says she gets the most satisfaction out of life when she teaches the functionally illiterate how to read. She says, "Zig, for the first time in their lives, the older ones are able to read the Bible."

You can be happy only when you do things for somebody else. Janet is a happy lady. She's a healthy lady. She's a prosperous lady. She's a secure lady. She has lots of friends. Her family relationships are absolutely magnificent. She has great peace of mind and tremendous hope for the future.

> "You cannot consistently perform in a manner which is inconsistent with the way you see yourself."
> – Dr. Joyce Brothers

Let me say it again: if you don't like where you are, don't worry. You're not stuck where you are. Janet McBarron read, she listened, she studied, and she took action. She did something for others.

In Helen Keller's autobiography, she records endless days of anticipation and despair, waiting for someone to draw her out. Then, she recounts the day she first met Anne Sullivan. "I learned a great many new words that day. I do not remember what they all were, but I do know that 'mother, father, sister, teacher' were among them. Words that were to make the world blossom for me like Aaron's rod with flowers. It would have been difficult to find a happier child than I was as I lay in my bed at the close of that eventful day and lived over the joys it had brought me. For the first time, I longed for a new day to come."

To build that healthy self-image requires you to know you are not stuck. You can grow. You can change. And when that self-image is solid, you'll be happier with your mate, your child, your job, and your neighborhood. If you find a lot of fault with yourself, it's easy to find fault with everything else.

My friend and fellow speaker Mamie McCullough says, "Every time you look at your hand, you should concentrate on your thumb. You should look at your thumb and remember you really are 'Thum-body.'" This might be a little silly, but you know, after I heard her say that, I am reminded of it every time I look at my thumb.

I've talked about immigrants, handicapped, minorities, senior citizens, the educated, and the uneducated. Now, what I'm going to say is aimed primarily at the 150 million Americans who, at least occasionally, read their Bible and go to church. I want to say this: some preachers in the past have probably tried to make you feel guilty about being successful. I want to deal with that.

I challenge all of you to take a sheet of paper and separate it into three parts. In the first column, write "BE." In the second column, write "DO." In the third column, write "HAVE." You will discover that everything you have is a result of who you are and what you do. You've got to be someone before you can do something; you've got to do something before you can have something. I challenge you to give me an exception.

Bible readers: who are you? Turn to the first chapter of the Book of John, the twelfth verse to learn who you are. What can you do? Look to Philippians 4:13 to learn. What can you have? Look to Romans 8:17 to understand.

Now, as I talk about this, let me tell you a couple of words that give people a lot of trouble. One of them is the word "deserve." I looked up the word "deserve" in the dictionary, and it says, "To be worthy of; to merit by labor or service." A laborer deserves his wages. A customer deserves service. When you talk about "deserve," do you really believe that Billy Graham deserves more eternal rewards than does the thief on the cross?

There's a difference in rewards here and rewards in heaven, but the question is still valid.

Now: what's a reward? According to the dictionary, reward means: "to give in return, either good or evil. Rewards and punishment presuppose moral agencies and something voluntarily done, whether it's well or ill." We read about rewards 150 times in the Bible. Look to Proverbs 24:20. Look to Psalm 58:11. Look to Matthew 5:12.

Bible believers, how does it make you feel when you hear a child say, "I'm a nothing; I'm a nobody. I'm a loser. Let's face it; I am just a nothing."

Does that make you proud? Does that get you excited? Do you say, "That's right, honey," or does it break your heart?

Do we have a right to criticize our Heavenly Father and say, "God, let's face it, You just made a mistake?" Folks, my Bible tells me God doesn't make mistakes. Ultimately, everything is going to work out.

# 3

# STEPS TO A HEALTHY
# SELF-IMAGE

I love this story of a 75-year-old gentleman. One day, somebody asked him, "Can you play the piano?"

He said, "Well, I don't know."

"Whaddya mean, you don't know?"

"Well, I never tried," the old man simply said.

Unfortunately, many times we automatically say "no" when somebody asks us if we can do something. In reality, there's a chance that maybe—just maybe—we could. Understand, I'm certainly not trying to shortcut the idea of training. But why would you say you can't do something until you have at least given it a try?

I love the self-image of this particular old fella walking down the street, talking to himself. Somebody stopped him and said, "Why you talkin' to yourself?"

"Two reasons," he said. "First of all, I like to talk to intelligent people. And second, I like to listen to intelligent people talk."

I thought that made an awful lot of sense.

## Building an Environment for a Healthy Self-Image

To build a healthy self-image, you must avoid certain things, like pornography. Psychologists say that three viewings of a pornographic film will have the same negative impact on your image as one of your own negative actions. When you see mankind at his worst, you experience a depreciation of your value of yourself.

I do not believe you can be an optimistic, morally sound person and watch the daily soap operas. The evidence I present is this: the Friday, March 26th, 1993 weekly summation of just two of the regular soap operas.

> **All My Children**: After Ryan and Dixie make love for the first time as husband and wife, they argue about her plans to go to Napa Valley to find Tad. When Dixie catches up with Tad, she accuses him of being after Noah's money. Distraught, Tad runs to Noah's grave where a vision of Noah tells him that Dixie needs him. He rushes to Dixie's side and stops her from leaving with the kids. When Helen walks in on Adam and Gloria in the midst of an embrace, she calls Gloria a tramp. To appease Helen, Adam offers to pay for Walter's funeral. Helen makes Gloria's day by telling her that

she is moving to Pine Valley. When Taylor overhears Mimi tell Lucas that she can't sleep with him anymore because she has chosen to be with Derek, Taylor runs to tell Derek. Lucas then must do his best to convince Derek that nothing ever happened.

And you thought you had a bad week before you read this! In one week, on one soap, we read about two-timing, fornicating, gold-digging, promiscuity, mysticism, distress, slander, appeasement, manipulation, lying, gossip, adultery, and bribery. How many of those are positive? If you think this description is just a rare exception, read one more.

**Days of Our Lives**: A videotape of the bogus Bo brutally beating Cash, in addition to Cash's identification, causes Bo to turn in his badge. Not satisfied, Lawrence blackmails Phillip into broadcasting the videotape in the hope of completely destroying Bo. Upon learning that she doesn't have much longer to live, Vivian aborts her plot to kill Carley, but she has another plan in mind. Maryanna is taken aback when Rebecca, wearing only John's shirt, answers his door. Although rejected, Austin still goes to bat for Carrie with the Face of the Nineties Contest but admits on Jennifer's show that he is available. Victor finds out about Billie's forgery, but lets it slide because she is on cloud nine over her book contract.

> **Failure is an event,
> not a person.**

What did we read there? Resignation, falsehood, brutality, blackmail, revenge, forgery, murder plot, rejection, and deceit. What do you think? Is this list positive or negative? The kids today say, "Everybody's doing it." They're right. Everybody on television is doing it. But everybody in real life is *not* doing it. If television can set this as the standard, more and more real people will be doing it. I'm not just talking about fornication and adultery; it also includes revenge, violence, murder, thievery, and everything else. You are what you are and where you are because of what has gone into your mind. You can change what you are and where you are by changing what goes into your mind.

We need to remind ourselves that failure is an event. Failure doesn't describe a person. Churchill failed eighth grade English three times, and he had a speech impediment. Does that mean he could never be an outstanding writer and orator? No. He was an incredible statesman and leader. Failure is a part of life.

Did you know baseball player Nolan Ryan has probably lost more games than 99.9% of all of the people who will ever throw a baseball? But we don't think of him as a failure because he continued to come back and win. Roger Staubach has probably thrown more incomplete passes than 99.9% of the players who will ever throw a football. The same thing is true of Terry Bradshaw and Joe Montana. Do we think of them as failures? Not hardly! They kept on.

Did you know George Washington only won two military victories in the War of Independence? The British kept pushing him back, but he was getting stronger and stronger. Valley Forge, the toughest time of the war, is the victory that enabled us to win our independence. Von Steuben, the little Prussian general, worked to teach the soldiers discipline, close-order drill, military tactics, and formation. They became toughened and more determined than ever. That's what brought on the victory. Tough times develop us, and then we can produce those successes.

## Learning to Communicate

In order to build a healthy self-image, we also need to know how to communicate.

Communication is so enormously important. Vocabulary is the key to communication; but confidence is what we build communication on. I'm not talking about public speaking, having the ability to stand and make a speech. I am talking about effectively communicating with other people so that we can understand what is being said.

Your communication skills—your listening skills—are some of the most important skills you have. You must learn to communicate.

When I say "communication skills," I'm not specifically talking about speaking. But let me discuss speaking for a minute. The fastest way to dramatically change the picture you have of yourself is to take a good course in public speaking. Most colleges offer them. The Dale Carnegie people have an excellent one. Naturally, our company has the best one. You need to develop that skill of communicating.

Most people give those who can stand up and speak in public without collapsing credit for intelligence they do not necessarily possess. Don't let that get around; we want to keep that one quiet! If you learn how to stand up and address a group of people, what it *will* do for your self-image is remarkable.

Let me give you three fast steps you can take to become a better public speaker.

Number one: if you're afraid of talking to a group, don't talk to a group. What I do, personally, is talk to people directly. I've never met a person in my life I wasn't willing to talk to! Chances are, you haven't either. Talk to the crowd one person at a time. And if you've got an old sourpuss out there, don't think you've got to win him over. You have to seek out that person who is responsive and friendly. You have to talk to that friendly one. Get your support and encouragement from them.

Number two: do you recognize the names Alben W. Barkley or Arthur MacArthur? Are you familiar with a lady who was seeking the justice of the peace office in a small New York town? I mention these people because, as far as I know, they all died while trying to make a public speech.

Think about it: over twelve billion people have walked the earth. Only three of them paid the supreme price. Therefore, when you stand up to speak, the odds are four billion to one that, afterward, you'll be able to sit down under your own power. It's a safe bet, folks; it really is. More people get killed bathing than they do while public speaking. Step up with confidence.

My third little tip is this: we could lead an old Mississippi mule up on a stage. He'd walk right across. He wouldn't be the least bit concerned about the audience. If you lead a thoroughbred up on stage, however, I guarantee he'd be all over the place. If you get a little nervous when you stand up to speak, just remember you're a thoroughbred and not a mule. This will do a lot of things for your self-image.

Recognize the fact that nobody really looks like those TV models. An article in the *Dallas Morning News* pointed out that this self-image problem creates issues for a whole lot of people. Be fair to yourself.

## Making the Right Choices

You need to make the right choices to create an impact on your self-image. It's safe to say that most problems can cause a poor self-image. We retreat; we don't move forward. We don't do the things we are capable of doing. We sell ourselves short.

You need to make the right choice.

Let's talk about the growth process. The Japanese raise a tree. It's a bonsai tree. The bonsai tree takes years and years to cultivate and develop—it is an art. The trees are absolutely beautiful. The bonsai tree can be anywhere from 12 to 22 inches tall. It can be of a number of different species, as well. When the little tree pokes its head above the soil, they extract it. They tie off some of the feeder and taproots, and they carefully shape the tree as it grows.

There's a tree out in California called the "General Sherman." General Sherman is nearly three hundred feet tall. It's wide enough to drive two automobiles through it, side by side. Engineers estimate that if they cut it down and saw it into lumber, they could build thirty-five five-room houses.

Now, the interesting thing is this: at one time, the bonsai tree and the General Sherman were approximately the same size. Each weighed less than .003 of an ounce when they were seeds. But the bonsai tree had its growth stymied and stunted, while the General Sherman fell into the rich soil of California. It was nourished by the richness of the soil, by the sunshine, and by the rain. As a result, it grew to be a forest giant. Neither the bonsai tree nor the General Sherman had a choice. But you have got a choice. You can grow.

Tomorrow is a brand-new day. Yesterday is gone. We've talked about making friends with yesterday, about taking the important steps to forgiveness. When you make friends with yesterday, focus on what you can do today, and plan for tomorrow, accomplishments grow. You have a legitimate chance to be happy and healthy and reasonably prosperous and secure; to have friends, peace of mind, and good family relationships.

## My Personal Story of Growth

Note the following: "Your attitude, not your aptitude, will determine your altitude."

I'm going to share my own story with you now. I happen to believe that for most of you reading, my story is your story. With three exceptions, you and I have walked in the same pair of shoes.

> **Your attitude, not your aptitude, will determine your altitude.**

The first difference would probably be this: I have never lost a mate or a child, either through death or divorce. I do not know how it would feel to suffer that loss. How could I know the depth of your love and feeling for your loved one?

The second difference would be this: I have had somebody who loved me all of my life. My dad died when I was five years old. Times were very tough; six of us in the family were too young to work. Money was short. But my mother always had plenty of time to love my brothers, my sisters, and I. My older brothers and sisters also loved me. When I got married, I was incredibly lucky to have a mate who loved me. I can safely say that she loves me more today than she ever has. In turn, I love her more today than I ever have. I have four children. Each one of them loves me. I'm doubly fortunate that my three sons-in-law and my daughter-in-law also love me. I have been tremendously blessed in that area.

The third difference would be this: I've always been healthy. I've never had any emotional problems. I have never had any serious physical problem. I cannot truly feel the way it feels to have these problems.

But if you've ever been discouraged, if you've ever been uncertain about what tomorrow's going to bring, if you've ever been unsure about what you were meant to be doing, or if you've ever been broke, I can understand you. I have walked in every pair of shoes. In so many ways, our stories are the same.

I was raised in a little town called Yazoo City, Mississippi during the Depression. My father died on a Thursday, and my baby sister died the following Tuesday. We had five milk cows and a big garden. I was milking cows before I was eight years old.

I was small for my age. In those days, we didn't have "poor self-image" concepts. We called it "low self-esteem," or, more appropriately, "an inferiority complex." One of the manifestations of a poor self-image is that you're impatient; you cannot solve problems. For example, when I disagreed with somebody, I would rear back and bust him one! I never discriminated. Whether this person I argued with was bigger or smaller, whether he was black or white, I would just punch him.

As a youngster, I had a very strong inferiority complex. I went to work in a grocery store before I entered the fifth grade. I was just nine years old. I worked every afternoon after school and all day Saturday. In those days, I made 20 cents working from 3:20 in the afternoon to 7:00 at night. I earned 75 cents for working from 7:00 in the morning to 11:30 on Friday night. I earned a grand total of $1.75 a week. I know what it is like to need a dollar.

But I learned an awful lot of things. For example, my boss was a former schoolteacher. When I dropped a grammatical boo-boo, he always corrected me. He became a surrogate father. He had a big farm, and he used to take me out and let me watch him as he talked with the laborers. He showed me an awful lot of things by example.

I remember vividly one day when I was ten years old, a man came into the store with a promotional idea. I sat there listening to it. Boy, it sure sounded good to me! My boss never even considered it. When the guy left, I said, "Mr. Anderson, why didn't you go along with that idea?"

"Well, you know, I don't know a whole lot about what he was talking about," Mr. Anderson explained. "But I learned a long time ago that you can't make a good deal with a bad guy. If his word is not his bond, you better walk away."

I found that to be true all of my life; you can't make a good deal with a bad guy.

When I was twelve years old, I added a paper route to my everyday activities. On Tuesday and Friday night, I delivered the Yazoo City, Mississippi *Herald*. One night a week, I collected money for that *Herald,* as well. I was a busy guy.

The man who was running the butcher shop in Yazoo City at the Piggly Wiggly store was named Walton Haining; he wanted me to come next door and work with him in the butcher shop. I worked with him that last year I was home. Afterward, I got in the Naval Air Corps. Getting in brought me more confidence and good self-image than anything else that's ever happened to me. I got in towards the end of the war; very few were making it in. I'd always considered myself "below average," yet, I wanted to fly those airplanes so badly that I applied anyway. When I made it in, you cannot begin to know what that did for my image!

I was to report for duty on July 1st, 1944. The night before I was to leave, Mr. Haining, the owner of that meat market, took me aside and said, "Zig, the war is winding down. I know you'll be back in a couple of years. I'd like for you to work for me when you get back."

I shook my head. "Mr. Haining, I don't think I'd be interested in that."

"Well, why not?" Mr. Haining asked.

And I said, "Well, there's just no money in a grocery store."

He pulled out his tax returns from the year before. He said, "Lemme show you something, Zig. Last year after taxes, I earned $5,117 for the year."

Now folks, as we approach the 21st century, this doesn't sound like a lot of money for a whole year. But that was $100 a week. Back in 1944, you could buy three pounds of good bacon for 27 cents. You could buy a 25-pound sack of good flour for 55 cents. I bought a little jacket for 87 cents. One hundred dollars a week in 1944 was a ton of money.

Mr. Haining said, "If you will come back and work for me two years, I'll teach you everything you need to know about running a market. I will help you get your own location in another store. I'll help you get your credit established, and you can own your own business."

I couldn't wait! The next day, I was *so* excited I was going to go to war. I was going to get it over with, come back, work for Mr.

Haining for two years, get my own market, and earn $5,117 in a single year! I was motivated.

On September 15th, 1944, at 9:06 p.m., at the YWCA on State Street in Jackson, Mississippi, I walked into the YWCA for the first and only time. Standing over by the nickelodeon was the prettiest little auburn-haired girl I'd ever seen. Man alive, did I ever fall for her!

I went over to her. With an enormous amount of originality, I said, "Hi!"

With equal originality, she responded, "Hi!"

The courtship was on. When I first saw her, I wanted to walk over and hug her. I wanted to start kissing her right then and there! But if I had, I would have skipped too many steps. I can guarantee you: she would not have been my wife for the last 46 years.

I make that point for this reason. In life, there are a lot of steps. You've got to take the steps. That's why this series offers a lot of steps. This series is not an overnight thing. If you've been going down one path for many, many years, don't expect to reverse the whole thing instantly. One step at a time, you can do it. You can eat an elephant one bite at a time. You can accomplish some amazing things with the right foundation and the right steps.

I got in the Navy. I met that little Redhead. After that, a lot of things changed about my plans. In 1946, I was suddenly going to the University of South Carolina. Uncle Sam had sent me there as part of the training program. When they discharged me, I decided to go back.

In November of 1946, we got married. I was selling sandwiches around the dormitories at night to finance the marriage and my education. I bought a little grocery cart, and I loaded up the milk, the sandwiches, and the coffee cakes. I'd go through and sell them. I did extremely well during the regular school year. Summertime heat ruined my sales, however, and I had to look for something else to do.

The Redhead saw an ad in the paper for a $10,000/year salesman. We took that to mean Providential influence—they wanted a $10,000! salesman and we wanted $10,000 It just seemed like too much of a coincidence. So, I went down and applied for the job.

It was in direct sales, selling cookware on a person-to-person basis on a commission. I had to buy my own samples. They did not actually believe I could sell. They turned me down. It took me two full months to convince them they should at least give me a chance. They finally gave me a conditional chance. They said, "We'll put you through the week of training and, if at the end of the training we think you can sell, then we will give you the contract." They wouldn't even tell me what the commission was. They really did not think I could do it.

At the end of the week, they figured they had nothing to lose. They gave me the contract. For the next two-and-a-half years, all I did was prove that they had been right to start with. This doesn't mean I didn't sell a lot those first years, because I did: I sold my furniture, and I sold my car.

They turned my electricity out, as well. My telephone was disconnected. I went down the grocery line and ultimately had to put a loaf of bread back. That's when bread was a dime a loaf. I bought my gasoline 50 cents' worth at a time.

I will never forget the day that the old '40 model Studebaker I was driving quit running. Now, I didn't know why, but I thought maybe it was the points, and I don't understand anything mechanical. I stopped right in front of a mechanic's little shade-tree shop, and I told him, "Sir, my car quit runnin'. Lemme tell ya' 'fore you even raise the hood I've got 50 cents. That's all I've got to my name, but I sure need my car runnin'. If you would just look at it." Well, he looked at it and, sure enough, it was the points. He reset them and I was off.

When my first daughter was born, the hospital bill was 64 dollars. I didn't have 64 dollars. I had to leave and make two sales before I could even get my own daughter out of the hospital.

I know what it's like to be broke.

But remember: "Sometimes adversity is what you need to face in order to become successful."

Finally, after two and a half miserable years of this, I asked Bill Cranford, my sales manager, "Bill, go with me; find out what I'm doin'. Help me. I've gotta make some sales!"

Well, he went with me on a call. When it was over, I said, "Well, Bill, what do you think?"

"Well, Zig, lemme ask you: What are you sellin'?"

I said, "Bill, now, you know what I'm selling!"

"Yeah, *I* know! But don't you think you should have told that lady?"

> **Sometimes adversity is what you need to face in order to become successful.**

We went to the training room. He had an old Webcor wire recorder, and he recorded my talk.

During my 19-minute presentation, I "uh-ed" 187 times. I emphasize this because these days, I'm the "fastest drawl in the West"! You really can change. The other salespeople were putting on group demonstrations with food and a sponsor hostess. They'd bring in the food, give the hostess a premium, and sell to the prospect. I wanted to do that, but I had three basic problems. Number one: I didn't have the money to buy the groceries or the premium. Number two: I did not know the first thing about cooking. Number three, I had never seen a demonstration. With the confidence that generally goes with ignorance, I figured I could do it.

I heard of a Mrs. B. C. Moore, who lived at 2210 High Street on the corner of Colonial Drive. It was a white, two-story frame house with no air conditioning and no insulation. Even during this particular August month, it was brutally hot! Mrs. Moore had a set of our cookware. She didn't like it because she didn't know how to use it. I said, "Mrs. Moore, I'll make a deal with ya'. I will teach you how to use that set of cookware if you will invite in two prospects and buy the food for the demonstration."

She said, "It's a deal!"

She invited Mrs. M. P. Gates, who lived down the hill, her sister and brother-in-law, Mr. and Mrs. Clarence Spence, who were living with her while their home was being built, and Dr. and Mrs. M. P. Gay, a dentist who had a set of the cookware, as well. He didn't like it, either, because he didn't know how to use it.

I did the demonstration for them. Apparently, it was satisfactory. I didn't burn anything, at least. When it was over, Mrs. Spence made a five-minute speech. She detailed how tough times were, about how they were building a house, about how they were in debt, and about how they were struggling to make ends meet. My heart became heavy.

But she continued, "You know, I'm always in debt. We're always broke. If I don't go ahead and get this heavy, nice set of cookware right now, I never will. I'll take it."

Mrs. Gates took her cue from Mrs. Spence. She, too, made a five-minute speech. I don't know if they were trying to impress their husbands, their hostess, or me. She made the same speech but wound it up the same way. "I'll take it."

There I was, so broke that if it didn't cost just 50 cents to go around the world, I couldn't have gotten out of sight! Before me were two ladies with their money in their little hands, both saying, "I'll take it!"

What would you have done, under those circumstances? Write them up!

Scout's honor, I looked at my watch and said, "Ladies, I'd like the best in the world to sell you that cookware, but I can't. I've got another appointment, and I'm running late! I'm gonna have to go and see them!"

With two ladies saying, "I'll take it!" I said, "Oh no, you won't! I got somethin' important to do," and out of there I scooted.

When I got to that other appointment, they weren't even there. Here's my question: how many of you, in your dumbest, greenest day, would ever have done such a thing? I'm saying there is hope for you!

## The Day My Life Changed Forever

My whole world changed one day. I went to an all-day training session in Charlotte, North Carolina. I lived in Lancaster, South Carolina, which is about 38 miles south of Charlotte. I spent the day, and I didn't learn a thing. I got back home that evening. I conducted a demonstration and came home at 11:30. Our daughter kept us up most of the night. At 5:30 the next morning, the alarm rang.

I rolled out of bed by force of habit. I cracked the Venetian blinds and looked out. I said to myself, "Ziglar, anybody with bat brains won't get out there amidst all that ice and snow, driving a little ol' Crosley automobile without a heater! Don't be ridiculous!" I did what any intelligent person would do; I got back in bed. But as I lay there, the words of my mother came back to me.

My mother preached me a thousand sentence-sermons.

"When a task is once begun, you leave it not until it's done."

"Be a matter great or small, you do it well or not at all."

"Your word is your bond!"

"If your word is not worth anything, then nothin' about you or what you have is worth anything at all!"

When I had taken the job, I had agreed I would be at every sales meeting and every training session. Though I had done nothing in the business in two and a half years, I had never missed a meeting or ever even been late for one.

That early input in my mind forced me out of bed. I went to the meeting. There, my whole life changed. A man named P. C. Merrell was there. Mr. Merrell was my hero. He had set all of the company records. He wrote all of the training programs for that company. At the end of the session, Merrell said he wanted to talk to me privately.

On that day, I was thrilled to death that Mr. P.C. Merrell, my hero, was willing to spend a few minutes with just me. There were 21 other people there he could have talked to; he chose me.

The conversation lasted less than two minutes. He looked at me, and by design or by happenstance, he said, "Zig, I've been watchin' you for the last two and a half years, and I have never seen such a waste."

That got my attention!

I said, "Mr. Merrell, whaddya mean?"

He continued, "Zig, I believe you could be a great one. I believe you could go all the way to the top. I believe you could become a national champion. I believe, Zig, that if you really recognized your own ability and went to work on a regular schedule, that someday you could be an executive in this company."

Please understand. He was talking to a little guy from a little town who was going to struggle all of his life. I never thought I'd live in the slums, but I certainly never thought I'd have more than one suit of clothes.

I said, "Mr. Merrell, do you really believe that?"

He said, "Zig, I know it."

The picture of myself changed dramatically. A lot of people have gone farther than they thought they could because somebody else thought they could.

I want to emphasize two points: first of all, Mr. Merrell was a man of unquestioned integrity. I knew he was speaking the truth. I knew that was the way he felt. Had I thought for one moment that he was just telling me that to sell more cookware so he would look good, his words would have had zero impact. But knowing him and knowing his reputation, I believed him.

Let me emphasize the second point: his statement to "go to work on a schedule" is so enormously important. At this point, I knew how to get prospects. I knew how to make appointments. I knew how to conduct demonstrations and handle objections, and I knew the sales closes. The salesman was ready, but the man was not ready. Until you get the man ready, the salesman is not going to be ready. You have to *be* before you can *do*.

I had already been trained in the skills and techniques. Now, the confidence that builds a healthy self-image was becoming my own. When I left that meeting, I was floating on cloud nine. When I addressed the three couples at my demonstration that evening, I knew they were going to go ahead and buy. They never had a chance.

Let me emphasize something very important: I had not learned anything about selling that day. I learned a whole lot about myself. When my image changed, everything about me changed. I finished that year as the number two salesman in

America out of over 7,000. The next year, I was the highest-paid manager in the United States. Three years later, I became the youngest divisional supervisor in the 66-year history of that company. Today, ladies and gentlemen, whenever I make a talk, I always pray, "Lord, make me a P.C. Merrell in the life of the people who are there."

I travel a lot. I get to meet a lot of people. I seldom get to know anyone, and I'm the loser as a result. I wish I could meet and come to know every person who sits in my audience, every person who picks up one of my books, and every person who listens to my tapes.

If I could, I would look you straight in the eye and say: "You were born to win. There are twelve billion people who have walked the face of this earth; there has never been another one like you. You are rare. You are different. You are special. You are unique. You are fearfully and wonderfully made. You were born to win! But in order to be that winner, you have got to plan to win. You must prepare to win. Then and only then can you legitimately expect to win."

I think we all, as citizens, need to participate in every election, be it local, statewide, or national. If we don't participate, we have no right to complain about anything. We have abdicated the right to gripe if we've not accepted the responsibility of voting.

> **You are rare. You are different. You are special. You are unique. You are fearfully and wonderfully made. You were born to win!**

But this time, I'm going to ask you to cast a vote of an entirely different nature. I'm going to ask you to vote for yourself. Here's the process.

Imagine, if you will, that you can step directly into the polling booth of your own mind. Imagine that you reach up and pull the draperies. This is a very private affair. As you make this particular vote, you'll note one of the levers has your name on it, written in pure gold. It is bigger than any of the others. You reach up and grab the lever with your name on it. You pull it down, at once excited, motivated, and enthusiastic. You vote for you! When you do, you'll discover that long ago, God had already voted for you.

Remember: eternal arithmetic clearly shows that you plus God equals enough. Always enough.

# 4

# SUCCEED IN A NEGATIVE, CAT-KICKING WORLD

Let's talk about relationships. You see, a lot of people have difficulty with them. As I dig into relationship difficulties, I'll share some ideas that will help to build better, winning relationships.

Many couples start off strong. For example, I once heard this lady say to her friend, "You know, when we were first married, we got along wonderfully well! But then we left the church…"

## Whose Cat Have You Been Kicking?

A man named Mr. B called a meeting at his company one day. He told all of his people, "Folks, you know we've been doing well, but we can do a lot better than we've been doing in the past. I must confess that much of the difficulty has been with me. I've not been the leader that I am capable of being. I haven't set a good example. But from here on out, I'm gonna be here early, and I'm gonna stay late. I'm gonna take short coffee and lunch breaks. I'm going to be the example, and I encourage everybody to follow through. We can do so well at this company. We can grow so fast. We can do so much!"

It was quite an inspiring speech, and he really intended to do all of what he had said.

But folks forget those speeches after a little while.

A couple of weeks later, Mr. B was out at the country club having lunch. He forgot all about the time. Suddenly, he looked at his watch and realized he was due back to the office in four minutes. He hopped up and made a mad dash to the parking lot, did about 90 miles an hour down the freeway, and found himself under the long arm of the law. He got a ticket. Mr. B was absolutely furious. He got back to the office, and he was steaming!

"The very idea!" he said. "This man out there worrying about somebody breakin' the speed limit just a little bit. He oughta be lookin' for robbers and murderers and rapists and these people who're breaking the law and leave us tax-payin' citizens alone!"

Mr. B called for his sales manager in a loud voice. The sales manager came in, and Mr. B said, "I want you to tell me about the Armstrong account. I want to know what's been happening with it. You've been foolin' with that deal for three weeks. You should have closed it a dozen times. Bring me up to date."

The sales manager explained, "Well, Mr. B, I don't know what happened. I thought I had it. I thought it was all signed, sealed, and delivered, but at the last minute, it just came unglued. I lost the deal."

Mr. B's anger hit the ceiling. He said, "You've been my sales manager for 16 years. I depend on you to bring in business. Here we had the chance to have a big breakthrough. You blew it. Just because you've been here 16 years does not mean you've got a lifetime contract. You better replace that business, or I'm gonna replace you!"

The sales manager was even more upset. He stormed out of there and said, "This is ridiculous! For 16 years, I've been runnin' this company. Brought in all of the business. Had it not been for me, it would have gone bankrupt years ago. And now, just because I foul up one deal, he blames me!"

Mr. B. called his secretary into the office and said, "I want to know where you are on that Hilliard account."

She said, "Well, you know, I've been workin' on three or four other things at the same time. You said they took precedence."

But Mr. B was angry. "Look. Don't give me any lousy excuses. I want that account taken care of. I want those letters sent. Did you get them out?"

"No, I've been busy on the other tasks," she explained.

"Just because you've been here for eight years doesn't mean you have a lifetime contract. If you can't do better on these things, I'm gonna get somebody who can!"

The secretary stormed out. She exploded. "This is ridiculous! I've been runnin' this company for eight years. Hadn't been for me, we'd have gone bankrupt years ago. And now, just because I can't do three things at once, he jumps all over me. This is not fair! Much as I know about that sucker, who does he think he's kiddin'?"

Oh, she was really upset. She walked out to the switchboard operator. She spewed at him. "I got a half-dozen letters. I need you to send them. Now, I know this is normally not your job, but you don't do anything but sit out here and occasionally answer the telephone. I want you to know that if you can't send them, I'll find someone else who can."

The switchboard operator grew angry. Her voice grew strong. "That's ridiculous! I've been here over ten years. Matter of fact, I'm the glue that holds this company together! If it weren't for me, we'd have gone out of business years ago. They're not doin' a thing in the back but gossiping, talking, and drinkin' coffee. I'm worked to death out here, and then they load something on me and say they'll fire me if I don't."

When the switchboard operator got home, she was still furious. She got the letters out of her bag. Just then, she saw her 12-year-old son lying on the floor, watching television. Then, she saw a big rip right across the seat of his britches.

She said, "Son, how many times have I told you? When you come home from school, you're supposed to put your play clothes on. Mother has a hard enough time as it is supporting you and sending you through school. Because you've been disobedient, go upstairs right now. No supper for you tonight, and no television for the next three weeks."

That 12-year-old boy was upset. He hopped up and said, "That's ridiculous! I was doin' somethin' for my mother! She didn't give me a chance to explain. It was an accident! It wasn't my fault."

Just then, his tomcat walked right in front of him. The boy reached down and kicked the tomcat. He said, "You get outta here! You've probably been up to no good yourself!"

See, we could have skipped a couple steps if only Mr. B would have gone directly from the country club to kick that cat himself.

Whose cat have you been kicking? Has anybody been kicking your cat?

Are you ever waiting for the green light to come along, and just as the light changes, there's a screaming horn right behind you? I mean, instantaneously—no time elapses between the light changing and the horn behind you. You hear that horn, turn around, and say, "Can't you see we got other people in front of us?" It's got nothing to do with you. Somebody has been kicking that dude's cat all day long.

Do you ever go to a restaurant to get a cup of coffee? You sit there, and finally, you meekly hold up your hand and say, "Ma'am, could you get me a cup of coffee?"

She says, "Can't you see I'm busy? I'll get to you just as quick as I can!"

Then, do you snap back, saying, "You don't have to bite my head off!" or do you understand her response has nothing to do with you? Somebody has been kicking her cat.

Have you ever had a marvelous day? Everything went your way. If you're in sales, on this day you closed the big account and you got a lot of proposals out. It looks like it's going to be the best month of your entire life.

You make it home to your five children about an hour late. Your mate screams at you as you walk in, whistling and singing.

Your mate screams, "If you had been here all day long putting up with all this, you wouldn't be feeling so good yourself!"

This doesn't have anything to do with you. Somebody had been kicking her cat all day long. Remember: it's not the situation, but whether we react negatively or respond positively to the situation that is important.

## Emotions and Personal Relationships

We're emotional people. When we deal with others, can we manage the situation so those emotions don't control us or how we feel?

I've got to make a confession to you. Much of this message is aimed at myself because I need to be reminded. Everybody wants to be happy. Everybody wants to be healthy. Everybody wants to be prosperous, to be secure. People want to have friends, to have peace of mind. They want to have good family relationships, and they want to have hope. Now, much of that is dependent upon your job or your profession, and much of that job or profession is dependent upon the relationships you have with other people.

Relationships with people make a significant difference in your life. The job you have, getting that job, getting that promotion, and keeping that job are determined many times by the relationships you have established not only at home but also on the job. The reality is that people hire you and keep you on the payroll because of your productivity, but also because they like you. What can we do as individuals to make certain that that relationship is built solidly? Let me start out by giving you ten commandments of human relations. They're not originals. You'll recognize virtually all of them.

1. You speak to people. That's very, very simple.
2. You smile at people. It takes 72 muscles to frown and only 14 to smile. A smile is the first thing you notice about others.
3. You call people by name.
4. You are friendly and helpful to people.
5. You need to be cordial. You speak and act as if everything you do is a genuine pleasure.
6. You are sincerely interested in other people. You can like almost anybody if you really try.
7. You are generous with your praise and very careful about any criticism.
8. You are considerate of the feelings of others.
9. You are alert to give service. What counts most in life is what we do for others.
10. You have a good sense of humor.

The best thing you can do behind a person's back is pat it; the best thing to do when you meet somebody with a chip on his shoulder is to let him take a bow. Very elementary—and yet enormously important.

People want to be right. They want to be appreciated, and they want to be understood. The Department of Labor says that, of all the reasons why people quit, 46% of them do so because they do not feel appreciated. My ten commandments of human relations will help solve that.

All of us want to always be right, but none of us can be right every time and in everything we do. When you deal with people, always let them know you understand how they feel, that you appreciate their position. After all, we need to understand that we are all emotional beings. When you get down to it, it's the heart that really influences most.

Do you remember when the seat belt law was passed in Texas? Everyone was so excited, so motivated. People called into radio shows; people wrote letters to the editor. Everyone was excited about saving lives. You probably don't remember any of that happening, but you may remember all of the people who called in and said, "What is the government up to now? No telling what they'll be trying to tell us here next. I mean, it's a free country! If I want to fasten my seat belt, I'll fasten my seat belt." You probably heard a lot of those calls.

I have flown approximately four million miles. That means I've heard the flight attendant say, "Fasten your seat belts," several thousand times. All over the airplane, you can hear them clicking.

I've never heard a single passenger say, "I ain't goin' to do it. It's a free country. If I want to fasten my seat belt, I'll do it, I just don't want to. What's the government going to tell us to do next?"

Let me give you some interesting data. If you fasten your seat belt in your automobile, you are three times less likely to be seriously injured or die in the event of a car accident. If you're in the airplane, 30,000 feet in the air, that seat belt isn't going to do you one bit of good. In most cases, I fasten my seatbelt throughout the entire flight anyway. It becomes automatic.

There are a lot of things we do that can become automatic. But it's essential that we discipline ourselves initially.

Did you see the movie *E.T.*? How many of you logical, adult people cried at the end of the movie? You see an alien from outer space, not even a person, on a big screen, and yet you sit there, crying like a baby.

Are we logical? No way! After all, people don't act *logically*; they act *emotionally*. The best way to get along with them is to understand them and try to get on their side of the fence. When we do that, it improves our relationships.

We need to be more sensitive. We need to be more understanding. One of the ironies of life is that the least sensitive people on earth never recognize the fact. They're obnoxious and, on many occasions, defend themselves. They say that's just the way they are, like you should accept their boorishness.

This one-liner says it all: a personnel manager says to a young woman: "Sexist? Don't be ridiculous! We employ plenty of dames!"

We need to be sensitive to the way others feel.

Of course, we don't want to go overboard. We certainly don't want to let paranoia set in. For example, I read a story about a young boy enrolled in a new school. His mother, being a very sensitive lady, started querying him about the makeup of the class. Finally, she asked, "Son, are there any minorities there?"

"Yes, there is one black person there. An African American."

"Do you play with this person of African American descent?" the mother asked.

"Why, absolutely not!" the youngster answered.

His mother proceeded to give him a lecture on why he shouldn't be racist. She concluded by saying, "Are you going to be more cooperative and play with this person?"

He said, "No, Ma'am!"

"Why not?" she demanded.

"Mom! She's a girl!" the child explained.

## Dealing with Boorishness

Remember this: "When someone we love is having difficulty and is giving us a bad time, it's better to explore the cause than to criticize the action."

Some people are tough to deal with. They have barracuda personalities. But we also need to understand something about their nature. My friend and mentor, Fred Smith, says that when others are mean to you, in most cases, they do not want to hurt you; they, themselves, are hurting. Every obnoxious act, in many ways, is a cry for help.

Michael Lombardi, Morgan McCall, and Ann Morrison at the Center for Creative Research did some studies. They learned that most successful executives had, at one time or another, a boss who was impossible. They learned to deal with that impossible boss and get along with them. They acknowledged it was the impossible boss who made it possible for them to develop tolerance and grow, overcome obstacles, and attain their positions of success.

> **When someone is having difficulty... it is better to explore the cause than to criticize the action.**

They also said that these impossible bosses helped them to form their own best management techniques and procedures. They had dealt with a tough individual and were determined to do a whole lot better. They acquired patience and dealt with conflict constructively. They avoided destroying that relationship. They built the relationship, learned from it, and benefited from it.

What can we learn in our relationships with our bosses? According to these behavioral psychologists, it's essential to never forget that he or she is your boss. It is your job to do the work the way the boss wants it done. You are paid to do your job in a way that makes the boss' job easier. You are there to remove obstacles for the boss, not to *be* the obstacle. In other words, the responsibility really does begin with us. Management will judge you by how well you get along with the boss; that judgment will affect your progress. Working with or around a rotten boss teaches you how to set priorities, neutralize potentially explosive situations, and choose your moments.

Earlier I referred to a member of our speakers' bureau, John Foppe, and pointed out that John, since he was born without arms, has to solve problems creatively every day—more than you and I have to solve in a month. It is because of that creativity that he developed so much maturity so quickly. As a result, he is able to understand how people feel. Because of that, he is far more successful than any 22-year-old I have ever seen in my life.

Don't try to change the boss. There is only one person in the world you can change: yourself. When you change, interestingly enough, you can more effectively deal with other people. You need to remember not to let the way other people treat you affect or determine the way you treat them.

We all admire Helen Keller. Helen Keller was born a perfectly normal little girl. But very early, she was afflicted with this terrible disease that took away her sight *and* her hearing. As a result, her family petted and pampered and spoiled her. She became absolutely incorrigible, a little girl nobody could get along with.

The first day Anne Sullivan was brought into the household to work with Helen Keller, Keller literally picked up food and threw it on her, trying to scream. Anne Sullivan simply looked at her and said, "Little girl, you can act like you want to. You can be as mean and as obnoxious as you choose to be. But I don't see you in the same way you see yourself. I believe you were put here for a purpose. I believe inside of you there is enormous potential. I'm gonna love you so much. I'm gonna treat you in such a way that the potential inside of you is brought out."

Who's the big winner? Helen Keller, of course. We know her story. Anne Sullivan was the individual whom God used to make that story a possibility. Anybody who can treat people that way is remarkable. But the potential of the human being is astronomical. We need to be careful about the way we judge others.

I read this recently and was impressed with it:

When the other person blows up, he's nasty. When you do it, it's righteous indignation.

When he's set in his ways, he's obstinate. When you are, you're just being firm.

When he doesn't like your friends, he's prejudiced. When you don't like his, you're simply showing good judgment of human nature.

When he tries to be accommodating, he's polishing the apple. When you do it, you're using tact.

When he takes time to do things, he's dead slow. When you take ages, you're deliberate.

When he sees flaws, he's picky. When you do, you're discriminating.

When he reads the riot act, he's vicious and insensitive. When you do it, you're just being honest for his own good.

Isn't it amazing how we set those double standards? Rare indeed is the person who can weigh the faults of others without putting his own thumb on the scales.

Something to think about, isn't it?

## Allowing Growth and Maturity

When we hire young people in our company and they stay with us over a period of time, especially as we watch our children grow, we forget that they are growing and developing and changing and maturing and becoming more capable all the time. They are capable of doing so many more things.

I find amusement in this little clipping out of *Reader's Digest*. "My mother has always treated me like her baby. No matter what my age. After turning 30, I purchased a computer and learned to use it. Thinking I'd impress her with my skill and maturity, I sent her a well-written letter, complete with computer graphics, borders, and an elaborate typeface. I phoned to ask what she thought of the letter. 'It's lovely, dear,' she replied. 'I have it hanging on the refrigerator for all of the neighbors to see!'" Sound familiar?

One Saturday afternoon several years ago, I was coming back from an out-of-town trip. I stopped by the office to pick up my mail. As I did, I found Lisa Carpenter, who worked with us at that time, walking out the door. I said, "Lisa, what are you doing here on a Saturday afternoon?"

"Well, I just came by to pick up the supplies I need for the training session I'm conducting this afternoon," she explained.

All of a sudden, it hit me like a ton of bricks. We had hired Lisa when she was still in school as a part-timer. She was a neat, pleasant student and a very bright worker. But I had, in all of my travels, not spent a lot of time talking with Lisa. I had completely forgotten that she was one of the most capable speakers and staff members we had. I had not, in my mind, kept pace with her growth. This is one of the most serious mistakes we make in management, one of the reasons people seek greener pastures elsewhere. They say, "Well, I cannot get recognition and respect for what I'm doin' here."

Let me stress the following point: you treat people like you see them, and the way you treat people determines your relationship.

A number of years ago, a young lady went to work for the Hilton Hotel chain. She was doing quite well. She heard that Mr. Hilton himself was going to be a guest in the hotel the next day. She had never seen him, and she was nervous and uptight. She asked the other clerks, "Have you ever seen Mr. Hilton?" They had not seen him either. The woman was worried she was going to mess up if she checked him in.

The next evening, to her surprise, she got a call from Mr. Hilton. "When I checked in this afternoon, you were so professional and gracious. You were so friendly. I am delighted to have you as a member of the staff!"

She hadn't even known he had checked in! All day she had thought, "Maybe this is Mr. Hilton." She treated everyone like he was Mr. Hilton.

> **Your relationships will have a direct bearing on your job, health, happiness, hope, and security.**

Then the thought hit me. Why don't we treat everybody like they're VIPs?

Your happiness is determined more by the success of your relationships than any other single thing. Let me also say that if you're not getting along well with the people who are important to you, you are one miserable human being. Your relationships will have a direct bearing on your job effectiveness. They'll have a direct bearing on your health. They'll have a direct bearing on your happiness. They'll have a direct bearing on your hope and your security. If the relationships are not going well, you start finding fault with everything you do.

By now, you should be comfortable with the way you see yourself. You can easily adjust and properly see others. Remember: the way you see them determines the way you treat them, and the way you treat them determines their performance.

Nowhere is discipline more important than it is in the way we deal with people. When you meet somebody who's rude and nasty and obnoxious, the inclination is strong to bite back at him. But the future you have in a lot of companies is determined by that relationship. According to Executive Recruiters, seven out of ten people who lose their job lose it because they do not have the right kind of relationships; there are "personality conflicts." Basically, we now live in a self-centered "I want to be me, I want to be free" society.

Let me just insert a word here about the concept of freedom. A lot of songs have the refrain, "I want to be free!" But, if you take the train off the tracks, it's free, but it can't go anywhere. If you take the steering wheel out of the automobile, it's absolutely under the direction and control of no one, but it can't move.

The sailor only has freedom of the seas when he or she has become an absolute slave to the compass. Until you're absolutely obedient to the compass, you have to stay within sight of the shore. Once you're obedient to that compass, then you can go anywhere in the world the boat you're on will take you.

Therefore, when we become disciplined enough not to utter everything that's on our mind, when we control our voice, we can, in fact, have a better opportunity to get ahead in life. Do you *respond* to the way people treat you, or do you *react* to the way they treat you?

I love the story of the Berlin Wall. When it was erected, there was a lot of garbage and trash. The East Germans took a lot of that garbage and trash before the wall was sealed and hauled it over to West Berlin. Just dumped a huge truck full of it. The West Berliners got pretty unhappy about that and initially decided to haul it back. But wiser heads prevailed. They got together a massive truckload of food, medicine, and blankets, and they sent it back across with a little note: "Each gives what he has to give."

"What is in it for us?" you might ask. Let me tell you what happens when we adopt the kind of attitude I'm talking about. According to Norman Schiedel, a group becomes a team when each member is sure of his contribution so that he can praise the skill, abilities, and contributions of others. When you are comfortable with yourself, fear and prejudice go right out the window.

One of the most moving photos I've ever seen in a newspaper was a picture taken at the very end of the 1992 Army/Navy game. Army won that particular game. This particular photo showed Navy quarterback Brian Ellis. He had just thrown one last pass of desperation, and it had been intercepted. The photo showed him on his knees, his head bowed, with Army defensive back Cadet Gaylord Greene, an African American, standing there with his helmet in his hands and his face against the helmet of his fallen adversary. He was saying, "We just played a tough game, but underneath, we're on the same team. We're brothers." This is a classic example of what happens when prejudice is eliminated.

In today's society, service is the buzzword. You hear it everywhere you go. Service involves relationships.

Henry Ford said this: "A business absolutely devoted to service will have only one thing to worry about, and that's profits. They will be unbelievably, embarrassingly large." But the reality is that there are a lot of people who only give lip service to service.

Why is that? It's because you can't have service without a servant. And for whatever reason in our society today, a lot of people think that if you're going to be a servant, you've got to be servile. Nothing could be further from the truth. As a matter of fact, two thousand years ago, the carpenter from Galilee said, "He who would be the greatest among you must become the servant of all."

In my dealings around the country, it has been my observation that top executives have a servant's heart. They want to help other people progress and go ahead in their own lives.

Henry Miller said this: "Render a service if you would succeed. This is the supreme law of life. Be among the great servers, the benefactors. It is the only path to success. 'Give and it shall be given unto you.' Make society your debtor and you may find your place among the immortals."

Clinton Davisson said this: "If you want to become the greatest in your field, no matter what it may be, equip yourself to render greater service than anyone else."

Albert Schweitzer said this: "I don't know what your destiny will be, but one thing I know: The only ones among you who will be really happy are those who have sought and found how to serve."

## The Importance of Words

As I've said before, the words you use are important. The titles, the names, the way you address people are very important.

When our third daughter was born, we knew perfectly well we were going to have trouble with our middle daughter. How did we know? Our friends had all told us, and our relatives had all told us. They were absolutely right! It started the day we got home from the hospital with the new baby.

The neighbors and the relatives make a beeline for the bassinet, to the teeny little baby. Then, our oldest daughter would stand right there and hear over and over, "Oh, I know you're gonna love this little sister. You are such a big girl! I know you're gonna be an awful lot of help to Mommy." They really put it on thick for the new baby and the oldest one.

But what about that oddball stuck in the middle?

I handled this with sheer genius, if I do say so myself.

I would say, "Why can't Cindy (the middle one) be like everybody else? Why can't she be like Julie, our baby, and Suzie, the older girl? Why does she have to cry and whine all the time?" And, you know, kids do want to cooperate.

At that time in her life, I had given her a nickname: "Tadpole." When a neighbor came over, I'd introduce my children and say, "This is Tadpole." After I realized I was treating my children differently, I learned a few different words. I would say, "I want to introduce you to the happy girl in our family, the one who's always laughing and smiling, and just having a wonderful time. Aren't you, baby?"

And she'd look up and give me that little two-front-teeth-missing grin and say, "Yes, sir."

Now, one day, one of the neighbors came over. I said, "I want to introduce you to our happy little girl. Tell 'em what your name is, baby!"

My middle girl said, "Uh-uh, Daddy. I've changed my name."

"Oh? What's your name now, baby?"

She said, "I'm the happy tadpole!"

Family is so important—the language we use on them, the way we treat them. You treat people like you see them, and the way you treat them has a direct bearing on their performance.

Let me ask you the following question: can you take negatives and make them positive?

Most of the time, you can.

A few years ago, I addressed a Bay City, Texas, school on the "I CAN" course. At that time, they told me about a man named Barry Tacker, the disciplinarian. I don't know how many states have disciplinarians in their schools, but this one did—at least at the time.

Generally, when the children were called into the disciplinarian's office, they cried. They trembled. However, when Barry Tacker became the disciplinarian, he changed the disciplinarian game.

On his first day, a teacher said to one of the youngsters, "You need to go see Mr. Tacker."

"Wh…wha…what'd I do?" the kid said.

"I don't know, but apparently it must be pretty serious. You need to go see Mr. Tacker right now."

The child walked down with fear.

"Mr. Tacker, I don't know what anybody told you, but I'm not the one who did it! I plead innocent!"

Mr. Tacker answered him. "I've got several eyewitnesses that you are the guilty party. I wanted to confront you directly to see if it really did happen. If not, then I'll apologize and send you back to the classroom. One of your classmates said they saw you warmly greeting a new student in school yesterday and telling him how glad you were to see him in this school. Did you or did you not?"

"Well, as a matter of fact, I did! I did!" the child answered.

"Not only that, but you were seen picking up some trash on the schoolyard and helping a senior citizen across the street. Did you or did you not?"

"Oh, yeah! I did it! I did it!"

"Does your mom know what you're up to every day of your life?" Mr. Tacker asked

"Well, I don't know," the child shrugged.

"Well, she needs to know. I'm gonna give you this note. I want you to take it home and get your mom to sign it, noting that you have pled guilty to warmly greeting a new student in school. You've pled guilty to picking up trash, you've pled guilty to helping a senior citizen across the street. I want this signed and brought back tomorrow."

Do you think this approach is likely to get good results? What do you think the children thought about the school, about Mr. Tacker?

Behavior that is recognized and rewarded will be repeated. Whether it's negative or positive, if it's recognized and rewarded, it'll be repeated.

Think of the four-year-old who holds his parents hostage in the grocery store, kicking and screaming and demanding toys or some special food. The mother and father who are coerced ultimately are coerced again and again. Rewarded behavior, whether it's good, bad, or indifferent, will be repeated.

Now, the words you use make a difference.

Somebody once said that one picture was worth a thousand words. But that individual had obviously never read the Declaration of Independence, the Bill of Rights, or the 23rd Psalm. These are all words, but they paint such vivid pictures and give so much information.

Which words are important?

The most important thing you can ever say to a child is, "I love you." You can say to yourself that you "demonstrate" love with a home, with food, and with an education. But the kids want to hear the words. They want to hear, "I love you."

The second most important thing you can say to them is, "I made a mistake. Please forgive me."

A lot of parents believe those words would undermine their authority. However, nothing could be further from the truth. What you're really saying is: "I'm now wiser and have better judgment than before." There's nothing that pleases a child more than to know you are willing and secure enough in your role to say, "I made a mistake."

Other important words:

"I appreciate what you said or did."

"You are a big help!"

"That's a great idea!"

"Thanks for your input."

"What is your opinion?"

"You are important."

"Thank you."

Of course, the most important word is "you." The least important word is "me."

Remember again, people want to be right, and they want to be understood. And remember that the input in their mind is going to determine the output in their life. This is exactly the same within us.

I'm a great believer in putting in the good, the clean, the pure, the powerful, and the positive. Now, please don't misunderstand. When somebody is consistently doing the wrong thing and saying the wrong thing, you need to have one-on-one visits with them to explain the bounds in which they can operate.

However, I'm talking as much about attitude as I am about anything else. What is the tone of your voice? How many of you, when you were children growing up, heard your parents say, "Watch the tone of your voice, young man!"

What's more, have you ever said to your kids, "It's not what you say; it's the way you say it!"

One of the most fascinating stories I've ever heard involves the Bemba tribe in South Africa.

They're a very gentle and peaceful tribe. When a member of the tribe does something anti-social, they bring the whole village together and put the individual on trial. They have a big pow-wow in the very center of the village. The youngest person in the tribe who is able to express himself says, "Do you remember the night you held me on your lap? We were around the campfire, all of us talking and eating, and you shared your food with me."

An older child will approach to say, "Do you remember you were the first one who taught me how to bait a hook and set a trap for some game?"

An older child will step up and say, "Don't you remember, you're the one who told me how to find the trails in the forest?"

Every member of the tribe is called on to say something to this individual. This thing must be true; it must be positive. They must tell him all of the good things he's done. As a result, the following message comes in: "I can't believe a man or a person with all of these good qualities would do this anti-social thing you have done."

The records show that there is almost never a second offense.

Remember: "You cannot tailor-make the situations in life, but you can tailor-make the attitudes to fit those situations."

"As you sow, so also shall you reap."

Garbage in, garbage out. If you put the good stuff in, you'll get the good stuff out. How do you build winning relationships? You put a lot of the good things into them. You show genuine interest in the other person.

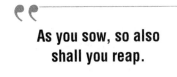

As you sow, so also shall you reap.

# 5

# COMMON SENSE IN HUMAN RELATIONSHIPS

Let's talk about building winning relationships.

Once, there was a man who married a lady who was a little bit older than he was. As a matter of fact, she was several years older. She was extraordinarily wealthy. For about five years, they had a wonderful time together. They traveled the world, lived in a huge home with swimming pools and butlers, drove luxury cars, and went to all of the best places to eat. It was wonderful for about five years. Then, she died. A few months later, a friend of the husband's said, "I know you lost your wife, but she left you in pretty good shape, didn't she?"

The old boy kind of smiled and said, "She did. You know, sometimes I miss her so much I think I'd give a thousand dollars just to have her back."

> **" I discovered that by enriching others, I enriched myself."**
>
> **– Sam Walton**

A lot of people don't understand how to be appreciative of other people. We are going to discuss this with great emphasis on the fact that you can have everything in life you want if you just help enough other people get what they want.

Let me specify something, though. This is not a tactic; it is a philosophy. Sam Walton put it this way: "I discovered that by enriching others, I enriched myself." The following applies to our personal lives, our family lives, and our business lives.

Let's first identify what it is that everybody wants. Everybody wants to be happy; everybody wants to be healthy. They want to be reasonably prosperous and secure. They want to have friends. They want to have peace of mind. They want to have good family relationships, and they want to have hope that the future is going to be even better. That's what everybody wants in life. What about applying this idea to their work life? What is it that they want, while there?

Somebody once said that perception is the cruelest form of reality. A study was done and reported in *USA TODAY* about what managers *thought* their workers wanted versus what workers *actually* wanted. They discovered the two were quite different. The managers thought the personnel wanted good wages, job security, and promotions in the future.

When they asked the workers the same questions, they gave entirely different perspectives. The first thing they wanted was interesting work. The second thing was an appreciation for the work they had done. The third thing they wanted was a feeling of being "in on things." The way we perceive others and ourselves is important. We need to know how others perceive us.

*Christianity Today* did a study of a very large number of ministers. They asked them, "How do you rate yourself as a preacher?" With regard to speaking ability, over 90% of them rated themselves at least average, and most of them rated themselves above average. The preachers went to their congregations and said, "How do you rate me, your preacher?" Over 90% of them rated their preachers as *average* or *below average*. We need to understand the perception others have of us.

What it boils down to, is employees want to feel important. I was appalled when the former President of the United States took an entourage of business people to Japan for the purpose of trying to get them to be nice to us and "let" our goods be shipped into Japan. Here's the scenario: a little nation, half the size of the State of Texas, with two-thirds of the land without a single use. They have no natural resources like iron, coal, or oil, and yet they are the number one creditor nation in the whole world. Here we are, the number one nation in the world, the most powerful nation, and we're asking them to be nice to us.

I'll be the first to admit there have been some inequities in the way Japan has done things. For example, they haven't had a huge defense budget, thus putting themselves at a huge advantage. Some of their laws are restrictive, as well. I was telling a reporter some time back that, according to the Harvard Business Review,

Japan will not buy some of our earth-moving equipment because the Japanese dirt is a little different from American dirt. They will not allow some of our medical equipment to ship there because the intestines of the average Japanese are shorter than the intestines of the average American. This reporter said, "Well, what on earth has that got to do with it?"

I said, "It has everything to do with it. It's kinda like the story of the fella who walked next door to borrow his neighbor's lawnmower. The neighbor said, 'I can't loan you my lawnmower! Didn't you hear? The flights from Buffalo to Chicago have all been canceled!' The first fellow said, 'What on earth have flights from Chicago to Buffalo, or Buffalo to Chicago got to do with borrowing your lawnmower?' The neighbor said, 'Not a thing on earth. But if I don't want to loan you my lawnmower, one excuse is just as good as another.'"

Basically, this is what Japan has done in some instances. They've created an excuse. As my mother used to say to me, "Son, there are generally three sides to every question. Your side, their side, and the right side."

Let me give you a little bit of data. Since 1974, American exports of automobiles to Japan have declined two percent. From 1974 through 1991, German exports of automobiles to Japan have increased over 700%. This indicates to me that the barriers can be broken if we take the right approach.

The Germans are very clever, as you know. They sent an entourage from Berlin to Tokyo. They caught a cab down to the Tokyo hotel, and they looked around for a day or two. Then, they caught the plane back to Berlin, and they said, "We've made an astonishing discovery! The Japanese drive smaller cars than we do! And would you believe it? They put the steering wheels on the right-hand side of the automobile. Now, maybe if we build smaller cars and put the steering wheel on the right-hand side, the Japanese would buy our cars!" They built the cars and, sure enough, that's exactly what happened. They said, "Hey! We like these automobiles. Send 'em on over here!"

What did the Americans do? Well, I saw an exciting article in the *Dallas Morning News* about current Japanese news. There was a showroom displaying the new Chrysler Jeep sold over there. The crowds were gathered around it; they were all excited about it. They were buying that car like crazy. They could not keep them in stock! Where was the sudden difference? Well, Chrysler did a very smart thing. They put the steering wheel on the right-hand side of the automobile.

You can have everything in life you want if you help enough other people get what they want. What did the Japanese want? Cars with steering wheels on the right-hand side. What did the Germans want? They wanted to sell cars. Help them get what they want, and you're going to get what you want! It really is not that complicated.

I'm saying it really does begin with us.

I had the privilege of being on a program with John Mackovic, the head football coach at the University of Texas. We were at a coach's clinic, and he made a simple observation. He said, "You know, when we've got the ball, I'm very much interested in the defense the other team has. But I know, deep down, that if I've recruited the right athlete, that if I have trained him and taught him as he needs to be taught; if I have developed a right plan of action, regardless of what defense they throw at me, I'm going to get my share of points." In other words, he's saying, "Hey, the action really does start with me!" I believe this is so important.

Why is Chrysler selling so many of those Jeep Cherokees? It's very simple. They took the initiative. I wonder how many Japanese cars would be in America today if the Japanese manufacturers had insisted on building the steering wheel on the right-hand side. I don't believe there'd be very many. In other words, we have to look at the other person and find out what they want. In relationships, what they want is not always what you think they'll want.

## The Bottom Line: Everyone Wants the Same Thing

Let's put all of this together. Everybody, whether you're the boss, the owner, or the employee, wants the same things. They want to be happy, healthy, and reasonably prosperous. They want to be secure, have friends, have peace of mind, and have good family relationships. They want to have hope.

Recently published UCLA studies have discovered, in essence, that if you have hope, love, and faith, your immune system is literally strengthened. Everybody wants to have hope.

What is it that the employees want? They want interesting work. They want appreciation for completed work, and they want the feeling of being in on things, a part of something bigger. In other words, they're saying, "Make me feel important."

Let's assume we know what the employers want. They want productivity. They want quality merchandise and quality products. They want loyalty on the part of the employee, and they want a profit.

Next, let's make sure the employer works to make certain the employee has interesting work and appreciation for work done. According to the Department of Labor, 46% of people who quit their jobs do so because they do not feel appreciated. One study by James Howard, a consultant of our company, asked the following question: "What does your boss or immediate supervisor say when you've finished an assignment?" The study revealed that 92% of people said their boss responded with, "Nothing." How does that make you feel? Does that motivate you?

Do you believe that if the boss provides interesting work, shows appreciation, and gives his employees the feeling of being "in" on things, then the employee would feel happy?

Do you believe your attitude and your happiness have anything to do with your health? If that were correct, the employer would give their employees a chance of being healthier, right? Do you believe that if they're happy and healthy, they're going to do better work, have a chance to get a raise, and go up the economic scale? In other words, their chances of prosperity increase. Does this give them a greater feeling of security, knowing that they're doing their job, and they're appreciated?

With all these things going for them, do you believe they'll have a positive attitude, they will be more outgoing, and they'll have more friends?

Does all of this really lead to peace of mind or help contribute to peace of mind for the employee? If you have a good job environment, do you think you'll have a more relaxed attitude and better relationships at home? In other words, when you leave to go home, if the boss says, "Good job!" rather than "Why, you lazy rascal!" it makes a difference, doesn't it? This improves family relationships and gives employees hope.

What has the employer provided? He's provided what the employee wants. The employee gets the benefit, here. But what about the boss? "I'm in this deal to make a profit, that's the reason I opened my business."

Remember the following quote: "Gratitude is the healthiest of all human emotions. The more you express gratitude for what you have, the more likely you will have even more to express gratitude for."

With all of these things going so well for the employee, do you think the productivity of the employee would go up? If the boss is giving you everything, wouldn't you want to keep a job like that? Now, what does the boss

> **Gratitude is the healthiest of all human emotions. The more you express gratitude for what you have, the more likely you will have even more to express gratitude for.**

want? The owner wants quality work. If the employee is getting these benefits, won't he be more likely to say, "my company" or "our company" instead of "the company" or "that company"? Isn't this the kind of employee who would be loyal to the company that they're working for?

Why is that so important? For the last seven years, according to Fortune magazine, Merck & Co. was voted the number one employer in America, the most desirable place to work. Seven years in a row. The magazine listed the ten things that determined this and Merck placed first in eight out of ten categories.

Why are we interested in that? Merck & Co. discovered that replacing a valued, skilled, and trained employee cost it the equivalent of one and a half years of salary. So, economically, it behooves the company to work with the employees to make them happy.

What does this do to the bottom line? Do you believe that the chances of the company making a profit are greatly enhanced through this process? You see, it is absolutely true that you can have everything you want if you help enough other people get what they want. It's important to understand that.

I love what Robert Updegraff says about this. He says, "In terms of downright happiness, the returns per minute from giving are far greater than the returns from getting." When we're givers, things happen.

In the business world, the number one quality owners and managers are looking for is the ability of each employee to get along with others. Why is this important? If you have one person who is a sour apple, if you have one person who is disgruntled and not carrying their part of the load, or if they create a lot of problems, then that individual will do tremendous damage to the company and bring the productivity down. As you well know, just part of the company does not go out of business; they're all in it together.

I was in World War II (even though I know you think I'm in my early thirties), and we used to laugh, saying, "Let's go sink the officer's quarters!" But the truth is you don't sink the officers' quarters.

## Serving Others Instead of Serving Yourself

Let me tell you one of my favorite stories. Two of England's great prime ministers were William Gladstone and Benjamin Disraeli. My two favorites, of course, have been Winston Churchill and Margaret Thatcher. I think they were two of the world's great leaders. Anyway, Gladstone and Disraeli were tremendously effective in their roles as prime minister. However, they had totally different personalities.

The story is often told about a titled English woman, a socialite, who was at a banquet one week with one of the prime ministers and the next week with the other. As was the custom in those days, they always paired them up: man, woman, man, woman. Society demanded that the man and the woman talk to each other. When the lady had dinner seated next to Mr. Gladstone, she was asked the next day: "What did you think about Mr. Gladstone?"

She answered, "You know, when I listened and talked with him, I became convinced that he had to be one of the brightest, wittiest, best-informed, and most knowledgeable human beings I have ever seen in my life. It was absolutely astonishing, the amount of wisdom and knowledge this individual had!"

The next week, after she has sat next to Disraeli, the same person asked, "What'd you think about Mr. Disraeli?"

She answered, "I became absolutely convinced that after talking with Mr. Disraeli, that *I* was one of the wittiest, brightest, most pleasant, and most knowledgeable persons on this earth!"

Notice the difference? Had the two been running for public office, which would she have voted for? No question about it, is there? Disraeli, right? Which one did she actually think was the smartest? Disraeli, of course! When you get wrapped up in yourself, as some people often have the inclination to do, you become a very small package.

Several years ago, I injured my right knee bowling. One of my friends, who's not overly bright, made a reference to my age. The reason I know he wasn't very bright is this: if he'd thought about it, he would have realized that the other knee was exactly the same age as the injured one. Nothing was wrong with it, so age had nothing to do with it!

Anyway, I was scheduled to speak the next night after this incident. About 3,000 were there. I walked out on the platform, noticeably limping. I could almost hear and feel the audience saying, "Well, look'athere! Ol' Zig is kinda crippled!

But I know he's gonna give it his best shot, bless his heart. I know he's gonna do his best!" Oh, I could feel it coming from the audience.

They put the microphone around my neck, then. I don't know the therapeutic value or the medicinal effect of a microphone around your neck as it relates to sore knees, but there's apparently some healing connection. When they put the microphone around my neck, my knee quit hurting. For the next sixty minutes, I was up and down, round and about, stoopin', squattin', shoutin', whoopin', and hollerin'. It went over well!

When I finished, I took the microphone off, I stepped down off the platform, and I hit the deck. My leg collapsed. Let me ask you a question: why didn't it bother me at all for 60 minutes? I think the answer's very simple. For 60 minutes, I was wrapped up in serving an audience. Then, unconsciously, I apparently thought, "Boy, I'm glad that's over! Now, Ziglar, you can think about yourself!" Boom! That's when I hit the deck.

About a hundred years ago, Andrew Carnegie, the first great industrialist our society produced, had 43 millionaires working for him. Now, 100 years ago, a millionaire was rich.

A reporter came to him and said, "Mr. Carnegie, how on earth did you hire 43 millionaires?"

He smiled and answered, "Well, when I hired them, none of them were millionaires."

The reporter went on. "What did you do to develop them to the degree that they became so valuable that you could pay them enough money to become millionaires?"

Carnegie taught us a tremendous lesson with his answer. "You develop people in exactly the same way you mine gold. When you go in a gold mine, you expect to move tons and tons of dirt to find an ounce of gold. But you don't go there looking for dirt. You go in there looking for the gold." Now, this is an interesting statement, because you really do find what you look for.

People are told all the time what they cannot do. They're so heavily criticized that they really don't know what they *can* do. They don't know what they want because they do not know what's available for them. Now, they can understand, "*You* could get it, but poor li'l ol' me? There ain't no way!"

## How to Build Winning Relationships

People who build winning relationships are what I call "good-finders." When we first moved to Dallas in 1968, I met one of the most fascinating men I've ever known. His name is Walter Hailey. He was in the insurance business. In those days, virtually all insurance was whole life. There wasn't much term insurance sold in those days. A million-dollar producer was a pretty good producer. A two-million-dollar-a-year producer was *outstanding*.

Walter devised a plan of marketing through mammoth grocery warehouses and independent grocers. The plan enabled his representative to sell ten, twelve, even fifteen million dollars' worth of life insurance each year. When I met him, he said, "Zig, I want to show you something. I want to take you over so you can see one of these mammoth warehouses. You won't believe how many groceries they can put under one roof!" And he was absolutely right. I didn't know there was that much food in the world!

We walked in the front door to find this huge switchboard and a lady who was in charge of it. He walked up to her and said, "Ma'am, I just want to tell you that you are the greatest on this switchboard. When I call, you make me feel like you were just waiting for me. It makes me feel so good. Just want to tell you how much I appreciate you!"

She said, "Why, thank you, Mr. Hailey!"

We walked down one of the corridors, to a little office. Walter said, "Just a minute, Zig. Let's step in here for a second." We stepped inside to find a gentleman. Mr. Hailey stepped up and said, "My name is Walter Hailey. I have not met you, but I have been watching your results. You know, we haven't had a problem in this department since you took over. I just want you to know how much I appreciate you."

The guy said, "Well, Mr. Hailey, I do the best I can!"

Mr. Hailey answered, "You're certainly doing a good job. Keep it up!"

We walked upstairs. We walked into Mr. Hailey's outer office, where we found his secretary. Walter said, "Zig, shake hands with the greatest secretary who ever sat behind a desk. I believe, and my wife believes, that she hung the moon! And you know, I'm just asking you right now, don't you ever take it down! I like it where it is!"

"Oh," the secretary said, "Mr. Hailey! You're mighty sweet to say that! Thank you very much."

We walked into his office. There sat one of his agents. Walter said, "Zig, shake hands with the greatest insurance salesman to ever put on a pair of shoes!"

The guy said, "Oh, Walter! You're just always full of that sort of thing, but I really like it! Keep it up!"

The whole trip took less than ten minutes. Let me emphasize something I've said before: you should never say something to somebody that you wouldn't say behind his back, whether it

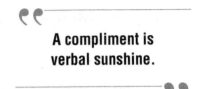

**A compliment is verbal sunshine.**

is good or bad. If you wouldn't give that kind of a compliment behind his back, then it's flattery. If the words are sincere, however, then a compliment is verbal sunshine.

How many of you believe, that as a result of those ten minutes, four people were more productive than they normally would have been? Do you agree that it's better to have one person working *with* you than to have three people working for you? When you form a team, you can get more done. That's winning relationships; that really is what it's all about. It's being thoughtful for people you're with and around.

A few years ago, in Dallas, I was speaking at an insurance company banquet. Two vice presidents and I were seated at the head table. I was in the center, and three other executives of the company sat to the side. The lady who waited on us brought us a salad. I half smiled and said, "Thank you."

A few minutes later, she poured the coffee, and I said, "Thank you."

A few minutes later, she served the entrée, and I said, "I'm just astonished that you're doing this so quickly, and yet you do not seem to be in a hurry. You're so pleasant to the people around you!"

She said, "Well, thank you very much! I appreciate you saying that."

When the vice presidents' coffee was poured, when their salads were served, when the entrée was delivered, they didn't even grunt. They didn't say anything. Finally, it was time for dessert. The dessert was a chocolate sundae. In a nutshell, that chocolate sundae was a scoop of ice cream with some chocolate syrup poured on it. The two vice presidents received a scoop of ice cream about the size of a golf ball. My scoop of ice cream was bigger than my fist! The chocolate syrup was running all down the sides. The vice presidents said, "Zig, you obviously know this lady."

I said, "No, I don't know her, but I sure know a lot about her!"

They said, "Oh? How do you know that?"

I answered, "Well, I recognized right away she is a human being, and there isn't a human being alive who does not genuinely appreciate a courteous, enthusiastic individual who appreciates the effort that they are rendering."

Now, don't misunderstand, I wasn't doing all that to get more ice cream. But again, you can have everything in life you want if you'll just help enough other people get what they want.

# Building Trust and Compassion with the Strength of Words

A story is told of a fellow who was given a tour of Heaven and Hell so he could make a decision about how he wanted to live and what he wanted to believe, so he'd know where he was going to end up. He went to Hell first. There, they had set out an unbelievable banquet table. It was a block long. It had every delicacy the world has to offer: all the fresh fruits, vegetables, meats, and sweets. People seated at the banquet table simply sat, half-starved. There were no smiles on their faces, no laughter, no gaiety, nothing.

After that, he went to Heaven. In Heaven, they had exactly the same menu. Every imaginable thing. But there, the people were laughing and joking. They were well-nourished, having a marvelous time. They were singing. It was a wonderful place to be. The visitor said, "I don't understand. You have exactly the same menu, but in one place, they're happy, and in another place, they're miserable. What's the difference?"

He was answered like this: "Well, had you looked carefully, you would have noticed that a three-foot fork and a three-foot knife is attached to the arms of each person in each place. In Hell, each person was trying to feed himself or herself and could not. But in Heaven, each fed the person directly across from him."

I believe this is more than a parable. I believe this is life. See, in this life of ours, we live with an awful lot of people. Our ability to get along with them, to a large degree, determines how happy we're going to be. If you'll check the record, you'll discover that regardless of everything else, if you're not getting along well with the people who are important to you, you're not a very happy camper. If you look at it in the other direction, even if things are going terribly in every area of your life, if you're getting along with the people who are important to you, overall, you are a pretty happy fella.

I believe that the best relationships are built on trust, respect, and genuine interest in the other person. From time to time, you may be deceived if you tend to trust too much. But you're going to live in torment if you do not trust enough.

You can learn a lot from chess players and athletes. In chess, all of the parts you play with are out in front of you. In championship matches, very frequently, the chess master will get up and actually look at the scene from his opponent's side. Sometimes he can see it a little differently. That's a good idea. Try to see from the other person's perspective.

In athletics, you must analyze your opponent, find out where he's weak, and exploit that weakness. In life, in selling, in medicine, in management, in education, wherever, you determine where your opponent, your prospect, or your student is weak. You strengthen that weakness. You find out what their needs are. You help them meet their needs to do your job in the most effective way.

How do you build winning relationships? One of the things you do is you eliminate gossip. I once heard a fellow say, "I hate to spread gossip, but I don't know what else you can do with it!"

One of the things I try to do when somebody says to me, "Did you hear about…" is say, "First of all, let me get you to do one thing. If you don't want me to repeat this and give my source, I encourage you not to tell me. I forget who tells me what and whether it's a secret or not a secret, and it's too much of a burden for me to remember what I can tell and what I can't. You know me, I talk a lot. I go at 280 words a minute with gusts of up to 550. So, if you don't want me to tell, just do not tell me."

People don't like gossips.

When people don't like you, they'll hurt you if they can. If they can't hurt you, they won't help you. If they have to help you, they won't hope for you. If they won't hope for you, your victory is hollow. Dr. John Maxwell said this. I believe there is so much truth in it.

Do you want to build winning relationships? You need to remember that the microphone is always open and the lights are always on. Did you ever notice the number of "celebrities" who, after they were quoted saying something, say, "Well, I didn't know that was for public consumption. I didn't know the microphone was on." This sort of thing is pretty ridiculous.

Several years ago, I was speaking in Tulsa, Oklahoma, at a trade school. The media had learned I was going to be there. As I was speaking,

> **Love thy neighbor as thyself is like a natural law, almost like a physical part of the universe.**
>
> **– Albert Einstein**

roughly one-third of the kids were sitting on the edge of their seats. Roughly one-third of the students were reading newspapers or magazines, and the other third were leaning back, acting like they were going to sleep. That was a "cool" way to treat this big dude from Dallas who had come there, telling them how to do things.

When the television camera came in, the recording started at the very back of the room. The bright light on the front of the camera was on, and they were videotaping all the kids in that audience. The camera came straight down, on the side of the platform, and behind me, to record me talking to the students. In ten seconds flat, I saw the most amazing transformation in an audience I have ever seen in my life! The papers disappeared. The magazines disappeared. Everybody sat up straight. They started straightening their hair. There was a dramatic change in the way they looked. This offers a tremendous lesson.

I said then, "Kids, I want to observe something. A few minutes ago, many of you couldn't have cared less about what I had to say. There's a possibility that's still true. But all of a sudden, you are very concerned about your image. Your image is not a thing in the world; it's the way you really are. Sooner or later, it's going to show itself. You can fool people some of the time. You can fool the boss, you can even fool the people around you. As employers, however, I can tell you that you will never fool the people below you. They see you, warts and all. They see the good parts and the bad parts. You'll want to remember that the lights are always on, and the mic is always open. If you keep that in mind, then you'll go further in life."

Out of *The Wall Street Journal,* we read *The Snake that Poisons Everybody.* It topples governments, wrecks marriages, ruins careers, busts reputations, and causes heartaches, nightmares, indigestion, and strong suspicion. It generates grief, and it dispatches innocent people to cry into their pillows. Even its name hisses; it is called *gossip.*

I love this about gossip as well: "I am an office mystery. I'm never seen, but I'm everywhere. I'm always on the job and often forecast important events. I make and unmake morals, reputation, and cooperation, but I'm seldom blamed for my mistakes. I have no responsibilities, and I am one of the most powerful molders of opinion. I add humor and anger to the office, and I pass with the speed of sound. I am basic in human nature, and you must accept me. I grow right behind you. I am the office grapevine." How true.

The words we use are so important in life. Above all things, we need to make sure our hearts and our attitudes are right.

Here is the story of a young woman and her mother. The daughter's close friend, Linda, showed up in the long driveway. The daughter said, "Linda is so slender. I just hate her!"

The mother said, "Come on! You know perfectly well there's something you can do about that!"

The daughter said, "There sure is! Hey, Linda!" She called. "Sure glad to see you! I've been saving you a big piece of chocolate cake!"

This is not exactly the approach I had in mind.

How important are relationships? God issued two commandments on which He hung all law and prophets. One: love God. Two: love your neighbor as yourself.

Albert Einstein put it this way: Love thy neighbor as thyself is like a natural law, almost like a physical part of the universe.

How important are words?

Several years ago, the Redhead and I were at a little resort area not far from here. It was a weekend. We were scheduled to play golf. We teed off at around 1:30. As it often happens on holiday weekends, things were backed up with many delays. I knew we'd be at least thirty minutes late.

We putted and piddled around until tee-off. There was one foursome in front of us. The Redhead and I stood waiting for them. This young, six-foot, four-inch Adonis was on the tee box. Weighed about 240 pounds, had about a 48-inch chest and a 31-inch waist. The kind of guy you could instantly dislike. He had muscles in places I don't even have places!

He stepped up to the tee, and he teed his ball up. He took his driver and he laid it down. Then, he picked it up again. This continued. Finally, I turned to the Redhead and said, "That guy's not a golfer, that's for sure!"

She said, "How do you know?"

"Aw, come on, sweetheart!" I answered. "I've been playin' golf a long time. I've seen a lot of golfers, and I can tell you: that dude is not a golfer!"

After what seemed like *forever*, he drew the club back, and he busted that sucker about 250 yards, right down the middle. Well, so much for my golf expertise.

The man then walked to his cart, put his glove in his bag, and walked straight back to me. "Mr. Ziglar, I heard what you said when you spoke in our community about two years ago. It completely changed my life. I want you to know it's just an honor to be on the same golf course with you."

I don't need to tell you that I felt about two inches tall. The thought occurred to me right then and there, as I asked for forgiveness, that my impact would have been very different if he had heard what I'd said on the golf course, instead. Folks, our words are enormously important. We need to be very careful about what we say to and about other people.

One of the men I admire and respect a great deal is Rabbi Daniel Lapin. He's a person I speak with often about the theological aspects of my seminars. I never record, speak, or write until I've checked something out psychologically, theologically, and physiologically, because we are physical, mental, and spiritual beings. Unless we put them all together, we put ourselves at too big a risk of error.

Rabbi Lapin has this to say in his publication *Thought Tool*. "If we listen as others are maligned, in spite of our disinclination to believe what we hear, our relationship with a vilified individual is forever altered. In other words, we are involuntarily influenced by everything we hear. 'Harmless gossip' does not exist. Listening to gossip can even leave us feeling dissatisfied with our spouse, children, employees, friends, and our life in general. Speaking gossip usually leaves us feeling less worthy. Words penetrate to our souls and cannot be erased or ignored."

In the Old Testament, in Leviticus 19:14, it says, "Thou shalt not curse a deaf man."

Well now, if a deaf man can't hear, what's the damage? The damage is what is done to the individual who utters those words. Acid destroys the vessel that contains it.

# 6

# HELPING OTHER PEOPLE GET WHAT THEY WANT

Do you remember when the Pope made his tour of America and went to San Antonio? Many people don't know this, but the Pope loves to drive cars. He had never driven a fancy limousine, and, obviously, they had the very best limousine for him. He'd been chauffeured everywhere. When it came time for him to leave, to go back to the airport to catch the plane, he told the chauffeur, "You know, I've never driven one of these. Let me drive." The chauffeur tried to talk him out of it, but he said, "No. I'm an excellent driver, and I want to drive."

He was an excellent driver all right, but he did drive a little fast. He got out on the freeway, and he had that sucker really going fast. He heard the siren behind him and saw the flashing lights. He pulled over to the side, and the patrolman walked up. He took one look at the Pope and said, "'Scuse me." He went back to his patrol car and called headquarters, saying, "Hey, we got a serious problem!"

"What's the problem?" they asked.

"We got a big one!" was all the patrolman could say.

"Well, is it the Mayor?"

"Oh, no! He's bigger'n that!"

"Is it the Governor?"

"Oh, no! He's lots bigger than that!"

"Well, how big is he?"

"I don't know, but he's gotta be a big one! He's got the Pope as his chauffeur!"

## Helping People Along the Way

In life, there are a lot of important people. But let's explore the philosophy of this statement I've made quite a few times already: You can have everything in life you want if you'll help enough other people get what they want.

How does it work in the corporate world?

You might say, "Wait a minute, Zig! I work on Main Street; I deal with Wall Street."

I challenge you to pick up an issue of the December 8th, 1989 issue of *The Wall Street Journal*. In this issue, they talk about the Golden Rule Companies. "Do unto others as you want them to do unto you."

They discovered something rather intriguing about these Golden Rule companies. Number one: these companies grow faster; number two: they make more money; number three: they have a greater return on equity than other companies.

Let me ask you. What kind of doctor do you want to go to? What kind of store do you want to go to? What kind of service person do you want to deal with? Don't you always want somebody who has a prime interest in you, who's absolutely honest, whose integrity is beyond question, and who you can absolutely trust? The reality is that these people and companies are more profitable.

In the December 1989 issue of *Executive Excellence*, there is an article by Ken Blanchard, otherwise known as the One-Minute Manager. Dr. Blanchard pointed out in this article that had you invested $30,000 in the stock market across the board 30 years ago, you would have earned roughly $109,000.

But, had you taken the same $30,000 and invested it in the 15 companies with integrity as the base from which they operate and an announced public policy, you'd have over one million dollars. With integrity, you have nothing to fear because you have nothing to hide.

We can tie this into the way we deal with other people. A number of years ago, just outside of Boston, Massachusetts, there was a mental institution. Although this one was ahead of

> **With integrity, you have nothing to fear because you have nothing to hide.**

most in the country, they still had a dungeon downstairs in which they put the people for which there was "no hope."

At this time, they had a little girl named Annie. Little Annie had tremendous mood swings. One day, she was kind, loving, and gentle, and another day she was a little animal. She was absolutely impossible to predict. They had to put her down in the dungeon.

An elderly nurse worked there who was nearing retirement. For whatever reason, she started going down to the dungeon and having her lunch just outside of Little Annie's cave. She wouldn't necessarily talk to her. She might speak, might say a few things, but she was just there every day. In her own way, she was communicating to her, "You are a human being. I do love you. I have an interest in you."

One day, she took some brownies and put them inside the dungeon, and Little Annie ignored them. However, the next day she noticed the brownies were gone. The next Thursday, she took some more brownies, and the process went on. The doctors noticed there was improvement in Little Annie. They decided they would move her up and put her in the treatment process. Later, they pronounced her well. They told her, "You can leave now. You're okay. You can function in society."

Annie refused. "No. You know, this has meant so much to me; it has given my life back. I would like to stick around for at least a few years and pay back by doing some things for others."

Many, many years later, when Helen Keller received England's highest recognition for a foreigner, Queen Victoria asked her, "To whom or what do you attribute your remarkable success in life, with all of the handicaps, all of the things you've done?"

Without any hesitation, Helen Keller said, "Had it not been for Anne Sullivan—'Little Annie'—this would not have happened."

Relationship building can go so far. You never know.

When I was a teenager, I wanted to join the Naval Air Corps. It was my dream. World War II was happening, then. I lived in Yazoo City, Mississippi. I wanted to fly those airplanes, shoot down the enemy, come home a conquering hero, and have a ticker-tape parade in Yazoo City, Mississippi. That was my dream.

I knew I had a basic problem. First of all, my grades had not been the best in school. As a matter of fact, I was in that part of the class that made the upper half possible, if you know what I mean. But, between my junior and senior year, I decided I was going to take summer school and pick up some extra math and science to prepare for the Naval Air Corps.

On the first day of class, I had to take a course in American History to get my high school diploma. This fact griped me to no end! "Why should I take this course in history? What good is it going to do me to know what happened a hundred years ago? I want to take math and science so I can learn how to fly those airplanes, shoot down the enemy, win the war, and come back home a hero!" I thought.

But I had no choice. They said, "You take the class in order to graduate. No high school graduation certificate, no Naval Air Corps."

I walked into that history class with a chip on my shoulder. I sat there and thought to myself, "Well, I'm going to get enough out of this to pass, and that'll be the end of anything I've got to do with history!"

Coach Jobie Harris was the teacher, and he threw me a curve. He turned into a salesman that day, and what a magnificent sales job he did! He sold me on why I had to know my history. I walked out of there a history major! The course was the only one in which I consistently made A's for the rest of my academic career. Today, my favorite subject is history. The best book I've read in the last 25 years is a history book, *The Light and the Glory*, written by David Manuel and Peter Marshall, Jr. It gives you the real story of America, and it's the most carefully documented and researched edition of anything that I've ever seen.

But Coach Harris did something else that day. He turned out to be a prophet who was way ahead of his time; it was 1943. He said, "Those of you who have an ability that goes beyond simply providing for your own needs have a responsibility and an opportunity to reach down and lift up those people who do not have that same ability and opportunity." Then, he finished it by saying, "As a matter of fact, if we don't reach down and help others, the day is gonna come when, by sheer weight of numbers, they're going to reach up and pull us down."

That's exactly what is happening in today's society. Standard of living, educational level, and everything else are on the decline. Our "I CAN" course, which is taught in so many schools, is a direct response to this effect. The financial cost has been substantial on our part.

Yet, I believe the course is one of the most important things we have ever done. I see youngsters today who tell me, "Fifteen years ago, I took the course. Let me tell you what happened." The work I've done in the drug war, in the prisons, and in the churches is a direct result of what Coach Jobie Harris said in that history class. You can affect people! You never know how many people that next one will affect.

The interesting thing, at least to me, is this: when Coach Jobie Harris was a youngster, he was a Boy Scout. His Boy Scout Master, the first Scout Master and Scout official in the state of Mississippi, was a gentleman named Thomas B. Abernathy. Mr. Abernathy, for whatever reason, took an unusual interest in Jobie Harris. Mr. Abernathy became a second father, a mentor to him. He taught him all about Scouting, but he also taught him a lot of other things.

Mr. Abernathy had four children, three daughters and a son. His youngest daughter is a girl named Jean. Jean Abernathy has been Mrs. Zig Ziglar since 1946. There is no way on earth Mr. Abernathy could have known that influencing Jobie Harris was ultimately teaching the boy who would become someone who would have such an impact on his future son-in-law, the father of his as-of-yet unborn grandchildren. You never know what's going to happen when you do something for somebody else.

The story is not over. World War II was winding down. They decided not to continue the flight training. I never even got to flight training; I remained in the college portion of it. The war ended, and I never got into the Naval Air Corps. However, if your son or daughter went to Corpus Christi today and became a naval aviator, one of the courses he or she would take would be our Business Development Course called See You at the Top. All instructors are required to take this course before they can train the young pilots.

The influence you have today, the good you do today is going to live on in others. Your attitude affects your relationship with your people; it also affects their income. The way you see them determines how you treat them. The way you treat them has a direct bearing on their performance.

> **The influence you have today, the good you do today is going to live on in others.**

## The Strength of Positive Thinking

Let me give you another classic, personal example of the power of positive thinking.

At age 25, after I finally got my start in selling, I became the youngest divisional supervisor in the 66-year history of the company. Now, in direct sales, in the cookware business, the field managers really control the destiny of the organization. Their daily contact with the salespeople, their training, their inspiration, their leadership, and their readiness to solve the problems give both guidance and direction.

When I was promoted to the position of divisional supervisor, I had to promote a person who was not ready and not qualified to move to the field manager's level, but I had no other options. So, it just had to be.

When I received the promotion, the division was going really well. Everything was really coming up roses! Almost immediately, however, things started to happen. One field manager had a heart attack that took him out of operation. One of the men had his big toe almost completely cut off. For the next four months, he was on crutches and largely negated. Both men's organizations went kaput.

One of the managers had an integrity problem, as well, which always brings difficulty. It collapsed. The one who had taken my place in sales did not have the experience; so, that organization collapsed as well.

Here's the scene: one month ago, we had a vibrant, gung-ho, moving organization, and two months later, it was really going downhill! A rumor began that the company was going to replace me. That, "I just could not handle it. I didn't have enough experience. I was too young."

I really had a pity party. "Why, I'm the good guy! I didn't have anything to do with that heart attack! I didn't have anything to do with cuttin' that toe off! I didn't have anything to do with the fact that I had no choice to promote that man. I had nothing to do with that integrity problem! Not my fault!"

I felt really put upon! "I'm the good guy, and they're sayin' those ugly things about me! That ain't right!" It was fast settling into a hardening of attitudes. I desperately needed a check-up from the neck up.

One day, in Knoxville, Tennessee, I walked down the main street to find a new book in the window. The title of the book was *The Power of Positive Thinking*.

I said, "Boy, if anybody ever needed some positive thinkin', it's ol' Zig!"

I walked in, picked the book up, and started reading it as I walked out the front door! I was on my way to the airport to catch a flight to Nashville, Tennessee, where I'd been scheduled for several months to speak to another division of the company about positive thinking. Wasn't this perfect? I was a guy with the worst attitude in the division, invited to speak on positive thinking.

This book, by Norman Vincent Peale, had been written specifically for me! He continually said, "Zig, I agree with you! You are not responsible for the heart attack. You're right, Zig; you had nothin' to do with the big toe. You're absolutely right, Zig, you had nothin' to do with the bad things, but lemme tell you what you are responsible for. You are responsible for the way you handle this situation. It's not what happens to you that's important; it's how you handle what happens to you that makes the difference."

Let's have a little reality check. Some people are so "positive," they lose their judgment. They think it's negative to even say, "Here's a problem!" Identifying a problem is not being negative. It is negative, however, when you say, "Here's a problem and there's nothing I can do about it. It's unsolvable!" Positive identifies the problem and says, "How am I going to solve this problem?"

Let me emphasize a point. The economy had not changed. The toe was still in bad shape, the heart was still in bad shape, the integrity was getting a bit better, and experience was gained day after day. Within sixty more days, we were doing more business than we'd been doing before all of those things happened.

> ...when you've got one stinkin' thinkin' leader, you've got an organization full of inept producers.

What changed? The thinking of the person in charge changed.

One of my favorite leadership statements is, "When you've got one stinkin' thinkin' inept worker, what you've got is one stinkin' thinkin' inept worker. But when you've got one stinkin' thinkin' leader, what you've got is a factory full, or an organization full of inept producers."

We finished that year 22nd out of 66 divisions. The next year, we were fifth; the next year, we were third. I'm talking South Carolina versus New York and Kansas, the only two states that beat us.

What happened? What happened is very simple. Instead of having a pity party, my attitude changed. I started analyzing all of the strong qualities in each manager, and the results were absolutely dramatic. I was so excited!

Let me simply say I received a big promotion. This was followed by a big collapse. I caught the PLOM disease—poor li'l ol' me disease—big time! I spread the stinkin' thinkin', and the solution was found in a book.

Yes, you really can have everything in life you want if you just help enough other people get what they want. I can guarantee this is going to become a tremendous part of your life.

## Improving Your Self-Image

A number of years ago, I ran an ad in a newspaper in Houston, Texas. At the same time, I ran an ad in Denver, Colorado. I won't identify what the response was or from which city. However, in one of them, the ad read, "Earn $20,000 a year." In the other one, the ad read, "Earn $50,000 a year."

I received 25 times more responses to the ad on the lower figure because most people during that time could not see themselves earning the higher dollars. The only difference in the ad was the dollar amount. Most people never see themselves as the capable individuals they are. This is why I spend so much time building that healthy self-image.

How do you climb obstacles? I love the example that shows the picture of the person standing at the foot of the stairs, looking out. The elevator sign says, "The elevator to the top is out of order. You're going to have to take the stairs."

I believe this is like life. The elevator to the top is out of order, and yes, you must take the stairs in order to get to the top.

I believe that winning relationships, that *friends*, are going to play an important part in your climb.

Aren't we all looking for friends? Don't we need that attention? Isn't it true, particularly within our families, that the things we do any Barnes & Noble Booksellers store for returns of new and unread books, and unopened and undamaged music CDs, DVDs, vinyl records, electronics, toys/games and audio books made within 30 days of purchase from a Barnes & Noble Booksellers store or Barnes & Noble.com with the below exceptions:

Undamaged NOOKs purchased from any Barnes & Noble Booksellers store or from Barnes & Noble.com may be returned within 14 days when accompanied with a sales receipt or with a Barnes & Noble.com packing slip or may be exchanged within 30 days with a gift receipt.

A store credit for the purchase price will be issued (i) when a gift receipt is presented within 30 days of purchase, (ii) for all textbooks returns and exchanges, or (iii) when the original tender is PayPal.

Items purchased as part of a Buy One Get One or Buy Two, Get Third Free offer are available for exchange only, unless all items purchased as part of the offer are returned, in which case such items are available for a refund (in 30 days). Exchanges of the items sold at no cost are available only for items of equal or lesser value than the original cost of such item.

Opened music CDs, DVDs, vinyl records, electronics, toys/games, and audio books may not be returned, and can be exchanged only for the same product and only if defective. NOOKs purchased from other retailers or sellers are returnable only to the retailer or seller from which they were purchased pursuant to such retailer's or seller's return policy. Magazines, newspapers, eBooks, digital downloads, and used books are not returnable or exchangeable. Defective NOOKs may be exchanged at the store in accordance with the applicable warranty.

Returns or exchanges will not be permitted (i) after 30 days or without receipt or (ii) for product not carried by Barnes & Noble.com, (iii) for purchases made with a check less than 7 days prior to the date of return.

*Policy on receipt may appear in two sections.*

Valid through 1/31/2022

# Buy 1
# Fresh Baked Cookie
# Get 50% OFF a 2nd
# Cookie

## Mix or Match any flavor

To redeem: Present this coupon in the Cafe.

Y4T8M8R

Buy 1 Fresh Baked Cookie Get 50% OFF a 2nd:
*Valid for Fresh Baked cookies only.*
*1 redemption per coupon.*
*Items included are subject to change.*
*Ask Cafe cashier for details.*

# Return Policy

With a sales receipt or Barnes & Noble.com packing slip, a full refund in the original form of payment will be issued from any Barnes & Noble Booksellers store for returns of new and unread books, and unopened and undamaged music CDs, DVDs, vinyl records, electronics, toys/games and audio books made within 30 days of purchase from a Barnes & Noble Booksellers store or Barnes & Noble.com with the below exceptions:

Undamaged NOOKs purchased from any Barnes & Noble Booksellers store or from Barnes & Noble.com may be returned within 14 days when accompanied with a sales receipt or with a Barnes & Noble.com packing slip or may be exchanged within 30 days with a gift receipt.

A store credit for the purchase price will be issued (i) when a gift receipt is presented within 30 days of purchase, (ii) for all textbooks returns and exchanges, or (iii) when the original tender is PayPal.

Items purchased as part of a Buy One Get One or Buy Two, Get Third Free offer are available for exchange only, unless all items purchased as part of the offer are returned, in which case such items are available for a refund (in 30 days). Exchanges of the items sold at no cost are available only for items of equal or lesser value than the original cost of such item.

Opened music CDs, DVDs, vinyl records, electronics, toys/games, and audio books may not be returned, and can be exchanged only for the same product and only if defective. NOOKs purchased from other retailers or sellers are returnable only to the retailer or seller from which they were purchased pursuant to such retailer's or seller's return policy. Magazines, newspapers, eBooks, digital downloads, and used books are not returnable or exchangeable. Defective NOOKs may be exchanged at the store in accordance with the applicable warranty.

Returns or exchanges will not be permitted (i) after 30 days or without receipt or (ii) for product not carried by Barnes & Noble.com, (iii) for purchases made with a check less than 7 days prior to the date of return.

*Policy on receipt may appear in two sections.*

# Return Policy

With a sales receipt or Barnes & Noble.com packing slip, a full refund in the original form of payment will be issued from

Barnes & Noble Booksellers #2083
3485 Tyler Street
Riverside, CA 92503
951-358-0899

STR:2083 REG:005 TRN:1534 CSHR:Bryan T

Changing The Picture: How to Stay Motiva
  9781613397466          T1
  (1 @ 17.99)                      17.99

Subtotal                           17.99
Sales Tax T1 (8.750%)               1.57
TOTAL                              19.56
MASTERCARD                         19.56
  Card#: XXXXXXXXXXXXX6612
  Expdate: XX/XX
  Auth: 013834
  Entry Method: Chip Card Tap

  Application Label: Mastercard Debit
  AID: a0000000041010
  TVR: 0000003000
  TSI: e800

A MEMBER WOULD HAVE SAVED           1.80

Connect with us on Social

Facebook- @BNRiversideCA
Instagram- @bn_riverside
Twitter-   @BN_Riverside

056.04B              01/27/2022  07:38PM

CUSTOMER COPY

within our family make such a big difference? Isn't it true that the applause of a single human being is of great consequence? Doesn't it affect our productivity, our happiness, and everything we do in every area of our life?

It really boils down to being interested in the other person. It really does. There's no such thing as somebody without value. Everyone has value. When we recognize and encourage that value, amazing things can happen as a result.

I want to close by telling you a love story. Now, this is a different kind of love story. But, this love story has a lot to say. This is a love story about the game of golf.

Nothing pleases me more than going to the hillside and teeing that sucker up. I rear back, and I hit that sucker as far as I can—boom! Then, if I can find it, I hit that sucker again!

But I found out a long time ago that both a slow game of golf and a fast game of golf, in reality, take about the same amount of time. It'll take you about five hours, including getting there, getting ready, and warming up. It'll take you about five hours to play and get back home.

I travel a lot, and at this particular time, I wasn't going to come home, kiss the Redhead and my son goodbye, and head for the golf course. However, I loved to play golf. So, I did something really bright. I bought my wife and my son a set of golf clubs. Everybody was excited about it except, of course, my wife and son. Graciously, they went with me for about five games.

The Redhead finally said, "Honey, I just do not like to play golf. It's too hot, or it's too cold; it's too wet, or it's too windy.

You're just gonna have to count me out." There went golf buddy number one.

At the end of the summer, my boy said, "Dad. I don't know how to tell you this because I know how you like to play golf. And Dad, I like to be with you, and I know you like to be with me, but golf is just not my game. I'll wrestle with you, I'll throw the football with you, I'll go fishin' with you, and I'll ride bikes with you. But, Dad, golf's just not my game. Count me out." Well, there went golf buddy number two.

For the next three years, there wasn't much golf in my life. One night, we'd been out to dinner. We were on the North Central Expressway with the old Dal-Rich Driving Range. We were riding past it when suddenly my boy spoke up, saying, "Dad! Let's stop and hit a few golf balls." My son is a smooth talker!

We stopped to hit a few golf balls. We were banging away, and all of a sudden, he said, "Dad, let me borrow one of your woods." So, I pulled my four wood out of the bag and handed it to him.

My boy choked up on it a bit, he reared back, and he cold-cocked that sucker about 40 yards further than he had ever hit a golf ball in his life. When he turned around, his smile clearly said, "Ziglar, you got yourself a golfin' buddy now!" It was the second most beautiful smile I've ever seen on his face!

The *most* beautiful one was a few days later. We were at the club, on one of the par fours. My boy took that four wood and busted that sucker right down the middle. The ball stopped dead center, right in the middle of the fairway, in perfect position.

We walked to the ball. My son took the five iron out, kept his head down, and smooth-stroked it. The ball took off over the green, landing soft as a feather about 40 feet from the cup. He was hunting his bird.

If you're not a golfer, this expression simply means that if he sank the putt, he'd have been one under par. This means he did well!

And so, I showed my boy how to align the putt, and I showed him how to stroke it. When he stroked it, he had zero doubt. It was in the cup all the way. When the ball hit the bottom of that cup, my boy jumped about six feet in the air. I grabbed him, and I hugged him. Man alive, was there ever excitement! We did a little dance for a couple of minutes. Then, all of a sudden, it occurred to me: I had a problem.

I was on the green in two, also. I was hunting my bird. I was only about ten feet from the cup. I knew that if I missed the putt, my son would figure I had missed it on purpose to give him the win. That would be a cheap victory, which is quite a loss. So, I determined to do the very best I could. That way, if I did miss it, I could honestly say, "Congratulations, son! You won it, fair and square!"

My best effort always includes a little Providential help. I aligned the putt as well as I could; I stroked it as well as I could, and the ball went to the bottom of the cup. Before I reached down to pick it up, I looked at my boy, and I said, "Tell me the truth, son. Were you pullin' for Dad?"

He was eleven years old. He'd never beaten his dad before. It would have meant a lot to him. He would have won the hole.

> **People don't really care how much you know until they know how much you care—about them.**
>
> **– Unknown**

Without any hesitation, quietly, but very firmly, he looked me right in the eye and said, "Dad, I always pull for you."

And that, ladies and gentlemen, is love. That's pure love. That's what we need more of in Dallas, Texas, and Portland, Oregon. That's what we need more of in San Diego, California, and Albany, New York.

Love is what we need more of in every home, in every county, and every state in this great land of ours. We need it between the parent and the child, between the husband and the wife, between the employer and the employee, and between the teacher and the student. We need somebody who is pulling for us to do our very best. An old saying declares "People don't really care how much you know until they know how much you care—about them."

When you pull for the other person, you hold a persuasiveness that is beyond belief. When you're pulling for your child, when you're pulling for a customer to buy because, deep down, you know it's for his benefit, and when you're pulling for an employee to perform better because it is to his benefit, you become instantly more effective, instantly more professional, and instantly more persuasive. Love is a tremendous persuader.

I was raised in Yazoo City, Mississippi. We have a family reunion every year. Because we're in Dallas, and the other members of the family live much closer, we generally fly to Jackson, rent a car, and stop by the grocery store to buy our contribution to that big spread. The other members of the family bring theirs, already cooked.

Several years ago, we stopped to get the food. We got a smoked ham and a smoked turkey, some little snacks, and a number of canned soft drinks. The cashier figured the amount for us. The Redhead wrote the check, and as she handed the check to the cashier, she automatically reached into her wallet to pull out her driver's license and several credit cards. As she did so, she said, "You probably want to see these."

The cashier never looked down from the check. She said, "No, in Yazoo City, the name Ziglar is all the identification we need."

I left there in 1943. She didn't recognize my name. She was talking about a mother, an older brother, and some older sisters who had left a legacy beyond price. Legacies are left through relationships. They are left by the way you deal with people and your basic foundation. When we build the right foundation, when our hearts are right, when we really do have an interest in others, when we live with integrity, then we can live and leave something that will last infinitely longer than we will live.

I think Dr. Jack Graham sums it up as well as anybody when he said, "Wealth is the total of what you have that money can't buy, and death can't take away."

I believe with all my heart that if you buy the ideas, you buy the concepts, and you buy everything we've been discussing, I'll be able to close this by saying, "Do these things, buy these ideas, follow through, and I'll see YOU—and yes, I really do mean YOU—at the top!"

For this last part of the How to Stay Motivated series about self-image and building winning relationships, let me encourage you to read this information over and over. I can guarantee that you cannot absorb it all by simply reading it the one time.

Interestingly enough, I've had many people over the years say, "You know, Zig, when I get a bit down, I pop in one of your tapes, and it always gives me a lift."

Why wait until you get down? Why not, on a regular basis, read this book? You'll discover that you'll find information you missed before, you will be inspired, and you'll be motivated to do a better job.

Read this book on a regular basis; follow the suggestions. If you do, I'll see you, and yes, I really do mean *you*, at the top!

# ABOUT THE AUTHOR

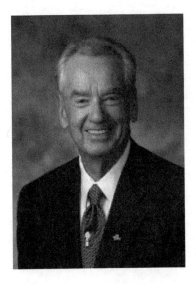

The late Zig Ziglar, a world renowned author and speaker, has an appeal that transcends barriers of age, culture and occupation. From 1970 until 2010, he traveled over five million miles across the world delivering powerful life improvement messages, cultivating the energy of change. Mr. Ziglar wrote over thirty celebrated books on personal growth, leadership, sales, faith, family and success, including *See You at the Top, Raising Positive Kids in a Negative World, Top Performance, Courtship After Marriage, Over The Top,* and *Secrets of Closing the Sale*. Nine titles have been on the best seller lists; his books and audios have been translated into over thirty-eight languages and dialects.

# OTHER GREAT BOOKS
# BY ZIG ZIGLAR